theatre & sexuality

theatre & sexuality

Jill Dolan

palgrave
macmillan

First published 2010 by
PALGRAVE MACMILLAN

Palgrave Macmillan in the UK is an imprint of Macmillan Publishers Limited, registered in England, company number 785998, of Houndmills, Basingstoke, Hampshire RG21 6XS.

Palgrave Macmillan in the US is a division of St Martin's Press LLC, 175 Fifth Avenue, New York, NY 10010.

Palgrave Macmillan is the global academic imprint of the above companies and has companies and representatives throughout the world.

Palgrave® and Macmillan® are registered trademarks in the United States, the United Kingdom, Europe and other countries.

ISBN 978–0–230–22064–5   paperback

This book is printed on paper suitable for recycling and made from fully managed and sustained forest sources. Logging, pulping and manufacturing processes are expected to conform to the environmental regulations of the country of origin.

A catalogue record for this book is available from the British Library.

A catalog record for this book is available from the Library of Congress.

10 9 8 7 6 5 4 3 2 1
19 18 17 16 15 14 13 12 11 10

Printed and bound in China

contents

*For the LGBTQ theatre artists who changed
my life, especially Alina, Deb, Holly,
Lois, Paula, Peggy, Terry, and Tim*

series editors' preface

The theatre is everywhere, from entertainment districts to the fringes, from the rituals of government to the ceremony of the courtroom, from the spectacle of the sporting arena to the theatres of war. Across these many forms stretches a theatrical continuum through which cultures both assert and question themselves.

Theatre has been around for thousands of years, and the ways we study it have changed decisively. It's no longer enough to limit our attention to the canon of Western dramatic literature. Theatre has taken its place within a broad spectrum of performance, connecting it with the wider forces of ritual and revolt that thread through so many spheres of human culture. In turn, this has helped make connections across disciplines; over the past fifty years, theatre and performance have been deployed as key metaphors and practices with which to rethink gender, economics, war, language, the fine arts, culture and one's sense of self.

Theatre & is a long series of short books which hopes to capture the restless interdisciplinary energy of theatre and performance. Each book explores connections between theatre and some aspect of the wider world, asking how the theatre might illuminate the world and how the world might illuminate the theatre. Each book is written by a leading theatre scholar and represents the cutting edge of critical thinking in the discipline.

We have been mindful, however, that the philosophical and theoretical complexity of much contemporary academic writing can act as a barrier to a wider readership. A key aim for these books is that they should all be readable in one sitting by anyone with a curiosity about the subject. The books are challenging, pugnacious, visionary sometimes and, above all, clear. We hope you enjoy them.

Jen Harvie and Dan Rebellato

foreword: Eros is in the house!

A theatre is the first place I ever had sex. Well, okay, actually in the dance studio of a theatre building at California State University, Fullerton. On my first day of college, which was also my eighteenth birthday, I imagined, hoped, prayed my queer boy's body would find another queer boy's body there in the theatre, and that is exactly what happened. I correctly imagined, perhaps even theorized, that the locus of the theatre was where I would find such queered bodies as Jill Dolan explores in her extraordinary *Theatre & Sexuality*. Dolan really sees how all the complex sets of exchanges in theatres are drenched in Eros. Whether a proscenium or a thrust stage – or my own personal favourite, a 'deep thrust' stage – we can no more keep the desire – queer and otherwise – out of the theatre than we can leave out the stale air, sweet wrappers, annoying ringing mobiles, or noisy programmes.

Indeed, even the language surrounding the audience–performer relationship is drenched in sex: 'They loved me!

They were begging for more! They lapped it up!' The site of performance is drenched in bodily fluids – saliva, sneezes, sweat ... not to mention the enormous lines at the toilet during the interval. No human secretion is without its moment in the followspot; I have personally bled at least a dozen times on stage!

Theatre & Sexuality charts the complicated disciplining and censorship of queer themes, artists, and bodies that have persecuted all LGBT theatre from the audience side of the footlights, from Oscar Wilde to my own NEA 4 freedom of speech case, which went all the way to the US Supreme Court. Dolan also shows how the queer site of live performing is inevitably drenched with oozing, powerful utopian libido that cannot be held back; it slips in under the doors and through the transom, totally liminal, a word that of course comes from the Latin word for 'threshold', the place where all the action jumps with entrances and exits. For even as desire motivates the subject and materiality of the content of a theatre piece, it also sets spinning the other relationships in the house – between the performers onstage, between the people in Row A and those in Row B, between the audience members and the bodies onstage – in a tango of charged possibilities of queer spectatorship.

Dolan has written powerfully in her remarkable earlier book *Utopia in Performance* about how live performance conjures short, precise moments and spaces where we imagine utopia, where we see its dimensions, where it allows us to sense what it tastes like. And one big piece of that utopia pie for me is the charged space of love, connection, orgasm, and joy rising up in new and deliciously queered formations of desire and embodiment that we constellate in theatres. In the sweaty heat of live performance we take a breath as the houselights fade on these stages, these seats, these wings where our love/agency leaps from Eros' bow and flies down Shaftesbury Avenue, through Times Square, and across Hollywood Boulevard right into our hearts.

Tim Miller is an internationally acclaimed queer solo performer. Hailed for their humour and passion, Miller's performance works have delighted and emboldened audiences all over the world at such prestigious venues as Yale Repertory Theatre, the London Institute of Contemporary Art, the Walker Art Center, Actors Theatre of Louisville, and the Brooklyn Academy of Music Next Wave Festival. He is the author of the books Shirts & Skin, Body Blows, *and* 1001 Beds, *an anthology of his perform-ances and essays which won the 2007 Lambda Literary Award for best book in Drama-Theatre. Miller has taught performance at UCLA, New York University, and the Claremont School of Theology. He is a co-founder of two of the most influential per-formance spaces in the United States: Performance Space 122 on Manhattan's Lower East Side and Highways Performance Space in Santa Monica, California. He can be reached via his website www.TimMillerPerformer.com.*

theatre & sexuality

Theatre & Sexuality argues that sexual identity provides a crucial perspective from which to consider how performance is created and received, as well as how sexuality is performed by actors and by people in their everyday lives. Considering sexuality as a component of theatre practice and reception allows critics and artists to analyse how performance refracts desire on both sides of the footlights. Although sexuality is as important as other aspects of identity – such as gender, race, ethnicity, class, age, ability, and other aspects of self-identification – it is not easy to 'read' onstage. How can we see, by looking at an actor, his or her sexuality or that of the character he or she plays? Must we rely on narrative cues in which a character tells us he or she is gay or lesbian or straight? Or can spectators see sexuality in an actor's gesture, his posture, or how she wears her character's costume? Alternative sexuality's relative invisibility productively complicates how spectators see theatre and challenges the artistic practices of actors, directors, designers, and producers. We often take for granted that what we see is heterosexuality. If we assume instead that not all sexual preferences or identities are 'normative' – that is, heterosexual, which is considered the norm – where do we look for alternative sexualities such as gay, lesbian, bisexual, transsexual or transgender, or queer, unless they are part of a play's content or are clearly assigned to a character? Conversely, how might spectators, directors, or designers 'queer' a performance by viewing it from such a non-normative perspective? Does it matter whether they claim to be gay, lesbian, bisexual, transgendered, or queer themselves? How does sexuality bubble underneath as well as within play or a performance, providing a motivating current of desire regardless of actors', directors', designers', characters', or spectators' sexual identifications?

Theatre & Sexuality traces the history and explains the critical validity of posing these questions to performance, placing playwrighting and production within the context of lesbian/gay/bisexual/transgender/queer (LGBTQ) social and theatre history. Critical attention to sexuality as a subfield of theatre and performance studies began as both a recovery project – calling attention to work by LGBTQ people that history had overlooked – and an interpretive practice in the mid-1980s and continues to flourish today. This book also honours the history of LGBTQ people in theatre who have identified as sexual minorities, whether openly or through the covert practices of the 'closet', focusing on the period since the 1950s, when sexuality became more publicly salient as an aspect of how people know themselves as subjects of their lives and of dominant or subcultural ideology.

Theatre and sexuality have always been productive spheres of overlapping influence, especially in contemporary Western performance. Sexual desire has long been a motivating narrative factor in plays and performances, the force that establishes or destroys relationships, that stirs jealousy and encourages infidelity, or that binds characters or tears them apart, regardless of their sexual orientations. Theatre is also a place of fantasy and longing, of fleeting exchange between spectators and performers. With its liminal status as both real and not, as ephemeral and transformational, theatre has long been a site where misfits and the marginalized have congregated. Sexual minorities have found among theatre people a generous acceptance sometimes not available in dominant culture's more constrained, conforming ways of life.

Theatre created from a consciously LGBTQ perspective ascribes politics to how it is produced, as well as to its content and form. For instance, many early LGBTQ theatres were collectives, borrowing the anti-capitalist and anti-authoritarian working structures of feminist theatre to displace the director's dominating power over the play's production. Ensembles such as the Women's Experimental Theatre, the WOW Café, Split Britches, the Five Lesbian Brothers, and the Ridiculous Theatrical Company (all in New York City), as well as Pomo Afro Homos (San Francisco), Bloolips (London), and Gay Sweatshop (London), boasted collective queer authorship and cooperatively devised performance. Thinking about theatre and sexuality, then, requires considering the embodiment of the actor and the spectator through a framework of non-normative sexuality. Each element of production comes into play: the text's narrative content, as well as its form and structure; the performance and its production style, along with those who craft it; and the audience and its relation to community, LGBTQ or otherwise.

The description of historical, critical, and artistic practices throughout this book will culminate in a reading of *Belle Reprieve* (1991), a performance collaboration among Peggy Shaw and Lois Weaver (of the US lesbian feminist performance trio Split Britches, which they created with Deb Margolin) and Bette Bourne and Paul Shaw (of the UK troupe Bloolips) that queers the canonical American drama *A Streetcar Named Desire* (Ethel Barrymore Theatre, New York, 1947). 'Deconstructing' Tennessee Williams' play (taking apart its form and content and revealing its operative ideology) was a historically apt choice for the Split Britches–Bloolips collaboration, as Williams' work was written at a moment in LGBTQ theatre history when the playwright's own homosexuality had to be disguised, in his plays and in his life. David Savran, in *Communists, Cowboys, and Queers* (1992), addresses how gay male sexual desire coursed between Williams' characters in covert and often displaced ways. *Belle Reprieve* exploded Williams' play with Split Britches' and Bloolips' interventionist theatricality. The production critiqued the original's realism with witty commentary, Brechtian acting, and a 'poor theatre' style that let the seams of theatrical illusion show. Through pointed, often bawdy humour, the performers commented on the obvious constructedness of their gendered and sexuality-based roles. *Belle Reprieve* was originally produced at the Drill Hall in London and opened shortly after at La MaMa E.T.C., the experimental theatre club (hence E.T.C.) and venue in downtown New York. By explicating the performance strategies and resistant reading practices that *Belle Reprieve* makes evident, *Theatre & Sexuality* demonstrates theory in action through performance and illustrates the pleasure that can be found in such critical approaches. The book also traces the interplay between commercial or 'mainstream' theatre, represented by Williams, and the more avant-garde, experimental performance generated by groups such as Split Britches and Bloolips. *Theatre & Sexuality* perhaps privileges the avant-garde, in part because earlier versions of the story of LGBTQ theatre in the USA, the UK, and elsewhere have focused almost exclusively on commercial theatre, where white men tend to be most visible and successful. By refocusing the story to look at the margins as well as the centre, I hope to tell a richer, more complex story about how sexuality has been represented and has influenced theatre from the twentieth century to the present.

Gay and lesbian lives and ideas in the twentieth century

Although it has provided refuge for people who deviate from heterosexual norms, theatre has also long been a site for dominant culture to clamp down on sexual minorities and to censor representations that suggested relationships or characters that weren't staunchly heterosexual. In the USA, the Comstock Law of 1873 enforced public morality by censoring materials considered 'obscene' and preventing the distribution of contraceptive information. The law also allowed vice police to close theatres in New York, in particular, for the slightest indiscretions. Edouard Bourdet's 1926 play *The Captive* (Empire Theatre, New York), which scholars believe was the first play about lesbians to be performed in the USA, was considered indecent. Vice squads closed the production after only a five-month run. In 1927, Mae West, the popular actress/playwright known for her sexually suggestive style, performed her play *Sex* on Broadway. She and the rest of the cast were arrested, and the production was closed. She later attempted to bring to Broadway her play *The Drag*, which concerned a group of cross-dressers attending a costume ball. Although preview performances were staged in the tri-state area surrounding New York City, the New York Society for the Suppression of Vice threatened to ban the play if West tried to open it in the city itself.

At the same time, historians suggest it was an 'open secret' – a term explicated by queer theorist Eve Kosofsky Sedgwick in her 1990 book *Epistemology of the Closet* – that many theatre people were lesbians or gay men. The theatre attracted iconoclasts, for whom the constrictions of daily life proved intolerable while the fantastical spectacle and seductions of theatre provided personal freedom.

Public disapproval, however, meant that many of these people couldn't claim the freedom to announce their sexuality openly. The American playwrights Edward Albee and Tennessee Williams, for example, achieved mid-twentieth-century Broadway success even while critics for prominent papers not so surreptitiously referred to the well-known if not directly expressed 'fact' of their gayness. British playwright Oscar Wilde's flamboyant performances of himself, evident in his cutting witticisms and flagrant sartorial style, made his own body a site for dominant cultural surveillance, which eventually doomed him to be tried – and convicted – for indecency in 1895. Historians describe theatre people from impresario Clyde Fitch in nineteenth-century America to Alfred Lunt and Lynn Fontanne, famous actors of the twentieth century, as leading cloaked lives of sexual non-conformity.

Although gay men and lesbians found community backstage, theatre often perpetuated conservative, normalizing values in front of the footlights, forcing queer artists to remain closeted. Even plays by writers known to be gay told stories that damned and demeaned characters whose sexuality seemed the slightest bit off-kilter. Williams, for instance, wrote horrific scenes such as the one in *Suddenly, Last Summer* (York Playhouse, New York, 1958) in which a gay man who's been seducing boys at a beach resort is surrounded by an angry mob of young men and dies from cannibalism, a gruesome enactment of the historical moment's hatred for homosexuals. Playwrights of some renown, including Lillian Hellman, enshrined the day's dominating opinions when they wrote stories in which lesbians and gay men killed themselves or lived lives of desperate isolation because of their sexual desires. In Hellman's *The Children's Hour* (Maxine Elliott's Theatre, New York, 1934), for instance, two young teachers lose the school they founded when one of their students spreads rumours about their 'unhealthy' relationship. When one of the women admits she does have feelings for the other, her distraught confession prompts her to hang herself. For much of American and British history, mainstream theatre produced by noted playwrights had no place for healthy, self-actualized gay men or lesbians.

The fortunes of LGBTQ people in theatre have changed according to the politics of history. In the USA, the homophile movement – which essentially preached tolerance for gays and lesbians and was the country's first expression of gay rights – made tentative incursions into civil rights in the 1950s, when gay and lesbian subcultures began to form in large cities around the country (see George Chauncey, *Gay New York*, 1994; John D'Emilio and Estelle B. Freedman, *Intimate Matters*, 1988). In the 1960s, as liberation movements gained ground, these sexual subcultures became politicized through identification with the political struggles of other minorities, especially women and people of colour. Although US activist groups such as the Mattachine Society and the Daughters of Bilitis organized sexual minorities to advocate for their rights in the 1950s, many historians locate the advent of the visible gay and lesbian rights movement in the 1969 Stonewall uprising in New York City's Greenwich

Village. Before the Stonewall riots, gay men and lesbians congregating in bars around the lower western edge of the city – long known as a bohemian haven for artists, including theatre people, and others who led alternative lives – expected to be regularly rounded up by vice squads, who raided the bars and nightclubs they frequented. Men and women had to make sure they were wearing at least three articles of properly gendered clothing; if not, they were arrested on vice charges. When the Stonewall Inn was raided by police on 28 June 1969, gay men, some of the bar's lesbian clientele, and drag queens (men dressed overtly as women, wearing clothing and make-up that let them perform femininity) refused to go obediently into the police vans waiting to cart them away for processing. Instead, with long-buried rage at the injustice of their plight, they rioted, breaking windows, throwing chairs, and otherwise resisting arrest. When word of this uprising spread, the LGBTQ liberation movement was motivated to begin agitating openly and more aggressively for equal rights and fair treatment. In the UK, a parallel history saw the 1967 Sexual Offences Act passed, which partially decriminalized homosexuality. What became a national movement for gay liberation spawned a number of non-profit organizations in the USA that work to change legislation and increase acceptance for gays and lesbians.

Theatrical street activism in the 1980s and 1990s

In the last decades of the twentieth century, LGBTQ social activism in the USA and the UK took a more radical turn, with groups such as ACT UP (AIDS Coalition to Unleash Power) and Queer Nation reacting against the assimilationist bent of US national organizations such as the Human Rights Campaign, the Gay and Lesbian Victory Fund, and the National Gay and Lesbian Task Force. The passage into law of Section 28 of the Local Government Act in 1988 angered British activists, as it legislated against the 'intentional promotion' of homosexuality and against teaching it as an appropriate form of kinship. In direct protest against Section 28, OutRage! formed in 1990 and began planning public actions to object to unjust practices against lesbians and gay men. The group's first action protested police entrapment of men cruising public toilets in Hyde Park. In a subsequent protest, a 'kiss-in' was staged at Piccadilly Circus against the arrests of gay people who dared to express physical affection in public. In the USA, Queer Nation also used grassroots, public performance-oriented strategies to rally communities of gay men, lesbians, and people now calling themselves 'queer'. Queer Nation, in fact, was at least partially responsible for resignifying the word 'queer', changing its connotation from a derogatory slur against gay men and lesbians into a rallying label for people across non-normative sexual definitions and practices. 'Queer' allowed the LGBTQ movement to grow ever larger, as even heterosexuals whose sexual desires aren't completely normative can affiliate under its purview.

In the 1990s in the USA, ACT UP and Queer Nation protested the government's lack of attention to HIV/AIDS research and funding, and insisted on non-normative sexuality as the key and positive difference for queer people. Unlike the older organizations, which worked through courts and legislatures to change minds and policy and argued that gay men and lesbians are 'just like everyone else', ACT UP and Queer Nation used street protest and in-your-face, more aggressive and theatrical tactics to call attention to LGBTQ issues and to claim their difference, not their sameness. In its heyday, ACT UP staged 'die-ins' and public funerals at the White House in an attempt to make palpable the costs of government inaction on HIV/AIDS. Queer Nation's tactics included staging kiss-ins and circulating representations of LGBTQ sexuality on lampposts and construction sites, and sometimes in the traditional media. Queer Nation rejected the conventional goals of the more established movement, arguing instead that fear around the AIDS pandemic had shut down the most important and liberatory aspects of queer culture, which, for these activists, included public sex and public visibility for LGBTQ differences.

Agitation for queer revolution, as well as for civil rights and assimilation into mainstream society, continues in the USA, the UK, and elsewhere. In the first decade of the twenty-first century, activism has moved away from HIV/AIDS issues, as the cocktail of drugs that keeps the virus in remission has allowed people with AIDS to live longer, more productive lives. Instead, some social activists have embraced the assimilationist strategy, shifting their attention to marriage rights and to allowing gays and lesbians to serve openly in the US military, once again pursuing the liberal agenda of the earlier movement.

By the first decade of the twenty-first century, LGBTQ people had achieved some degree of prominence and visibility in numerous areas of public life. Entertainer Ellen DeGeneres came out publicly as a lesbian in the mid-1990s, when the character she then played on television announced her lesbianism, leading DeGeneres to declare on the cover of *Time Magazine*, 'Yep, I'm Gay!' Numerous other public figures have followed her lead. While the closet remains a determining aspect of LGBTQ culture, the increase in public visibility, at least for white, upper-middle-class gay men and lesbians, along with social activism and legislative lobbying, has begun to change public attitudes. The popular lesbian MSNBC political commentator Rachel Maddow has been out (or openly lesbian) since her show debuted, and other public figures have also been willing to name their sexuality as an important but mundane aspect of their lives.

From T. R. Knight, who played the hapless heterosexual George on the popular ABC television series *Grey's Anatomy*, to Neil Patrick Harris, who also stars as a heterosexual character in the CBS television show *How I Met Your Mother* and maintains a well-respected career as a Broadway actor, to Wanda Sykes, the African American comedienne who recently married her female partner in California and performs opposite Julia Louis-Dreyfus on the CBS sitcom *The New Adventures of Old Christine*, to Jane Lynch, who plays the haughty, track-suit-wearing coach of the cheerleading squad on the very queer Fox Television musical series *Glee*, gay men and lesbians have become visible across the landscape of public culture. Early projects of lesbian and gay theatre and film criticism searched dominant culture for popular images just like these, proposing that simple visibility would result in increased political acceptance and LGBTQ power.

Theorizing how to see sexuality in performance

From the late 1980s to the present, however, academics producing scholarship and criticism, in conjunction with the social activism in the USA and UK, have posed more complex questions crucial to how we think about sexuality in theatre and performance. Is sexual identity something a person *is* or a set of practices that a person *does*? Are people born gay or lesbian, or are they fashioned by the influence of cultures and communities through which they move as they grow up? The foundational debate between 'essentialists' – those who believe sexual identity (and gender) is innate – and 'social constructionists' – those who believe that sexual identity is *made*, that it's never inherent but always formed through interactions with history and cultural circumstance, as well as through personal agency – provided the theoretical fulcrum for the early phase of LGBTQ studies.

While historians set out to recover the lives of LGBTQ people who had been ignored or wilfully forgotten by earlier scholars, theorists, many of whom were influenced by the French philosopher Michel Foucault's analysis of the operations of power, began to develop notions of gender and sexuality as surface enactments of ideology that change with the shifting mores of history. American philosopher Judith Butler's book

Gender Trouble (1990) was foundational not only to feminist theory but to establishing the field that became known as 'queer theory'. Butler proposed that far from being innate, gender and sexuality form in a constant, ongoing exchange between social dictate and personal resistance or acquiescence. She theorized that gender and sexuality are relational categories. Using a critical method known as deconstruction, she proposed that binary definitions such as heterosexual–homosexual tie us to understanding one through the other and that social power privileges the first term of the pair over the second. By considering the power that infuses these pairs as historical and changeable, Butler theorized that gender and sexuality aren't innate 'essences' but social constructions that can be contested and redefined.

In theatre and performance studies, scholars adopted Butler's theories to move beyond their initial search for positive images of gay men and lesbians in productions towards understanding how the theatre apparatus inculcates gender and sexuality norms. That is, rather than seeing theatre simply as a reflection of gay, lesbian, or heterosexual 'subjects' (people at once subjected to ideology and with the agency to author their lives), theorists such as Sue-Ellen Case, Lynda Hart, Peggy Phelan, David Román, David Savran, and I considered how theatre forms work with content to produce representations of LGBTQ people that reinforce dominant cultural impressions of not just who they are but who they should be. These scholars argued that theatre doesn't just reflect reality and that positive images of lesbians and gay men alone would not promote social change. On the contrary, they proposed that theatre creates what we consider reality by enforcing conventional notions of 'normal'. The theatre genre of realism came under particular scrutiny because of its tendency to represent a hermetic world, closed off by the 'fourth wall' that imaginatively separates actors/characters from spectators, who are encouraged to identify and support worlds framed by conservative ideology that tends to marginalize, demean, or, worse still, exile or murder gay and lesbian characters. These theorists proposed that even in plays written by gay men or lesbians, realism constrains the power and self-determination of LGBTQ people. In the realist plays of Jane Chambers, who was one of the first out American lesbian playwrights, for instance, the more promiscuous, less conventionally domesticated lesbian characters are moralized against or die. In *Last Summer at Bluefish Cove* (Actors' Playhouse, New York, 1980), Lil, the protagonist, is a womanizer who's spent her life chasing other women's girlfriends and never settling down in a coupled, long-term relationship. Lil challenges the moral propriety of her community. In the end, even though she finally meets the (straight) woman of her dreams, Lil succumbs to cancer, and her threat to the community is resolved with her death.

Queering the theatre

Queer performance theorists reacted against realism's conservatism by championing post-modernist styles and genres that refused to observe the conventions of fourth-wall domesticity. They popularized plays in which characters commented in a distanced, Brechtian fashion on themselves or the plot and in which the apparatus of performance was revealed – the lights, set, costumes, script, décor, and props, the architecture of the theatre, the arrangement of the seats in the house, the location of the theatre within a city or town, and so on. Strategies for showing the mechanics of theatre's production of reality included allowing audiences to see lighting instruments, building sets that didn't try to convince spectators of their reality, and reading or displaying stage directions as part of the performance. The characters often directly addressed spectators, refusing to observe the compact in which actors pretend spectators aren't there, sitting in the theatre, watching. These plays and performances became objects of fascination and respect for a new generation of LGBTQ scholars and critics, turning their attention away from the commercial theatre towards the experiments of the avant-garde.

In addition to form and how it determines the meanings of content, queer theatre theorists considered how sexuality influences reception practices. For example, does a spectator need to identify as LGBTQ to understand a play in which same-sex attraction is the content, or structures new, more experimental forms? Or can only LGBTQ spectators fully understand such productions? Is it possible for any spectator to 'read queerly', as cultural critic Alexander Doty suggests in *Making Things Perfectly Queer* (1993)? If sexual identity is a set of practices, as Butler and other theorists propose, perhaps all spectators can read theatre and performance through a queer lens, regardless of whether they identify as LGBTQ. Likewise, Doty and performance studies scholars such as Stacy Wolf, in her feminist and queer investigation of American musical theatre *A Problem Like Maria: Gender and Sexuality in the American Musical* (2002), argue that theatre texts can *be queered*, turning a word that was conventionally used as a noun – a state of being – into an active verb describing a practice through which spectators, critics, and artists can reread any representation from a queer perspective. In her analysis of *The Sound of Music*, for example, Wolf proposes that Julie Andrews, who played Maria in the musical's film version, has long been the object of lesbian desire and fascination. Reading Maria as queer allows spectators pleasurable resistance to the otherwise insistently heterosexual content emphasized in the musical's plot. Wolf suggests that Maria's marriage to Captain von Trapp is the least interesting aspect of the play and the film, and that Maria/Andrews (and Mary Martin, the stage actor who performed the role on Broadway) draws lesbian (and feminist) attention because of her strength as a woman, her relationships with Liesl and the other Von Trapp children (and the nuns), and her singing and dancing, which liberate her physically from a conventionally domestic middle-class life.

LGBTQ artists, in addition to writing new material from a gay, lesbian, or queer perspective, can use the verb form to queer traditional material. In *Belle Reprieve*, for instance, *A Streetcar Named Desire* is transformed into a post-modern romp in which each character is played by someone whose personal gender performance is at odds with the conventional expectations that structure Williams' play. By referring to a well-known text, the four LGBTQ artists who revised *Streetcar* focus attention on how traditional theatre delivers intact and without question dominant culture's definition of gender and sexuality (as well as race, ethnicity, and other identity factors). In the queering of *Streetcar*, the presumptions about gender and sexuality of Williams' play – that a woman should always be loyal to her husband; that a woman should never threaten the authority of the 'master' of the house; that hyper-masculine men are sexually potent and magnetic for women; that virility and violence are inextricable – are emphasized as ideas perpetuated by custom rather than trans-historical values that must be accepted as fact.

LGBTQ theorists also proposed that desire is a major motivating force, not just in gay, lesbian, or queer theatre but in any theatre production. Analysing how sexuality operates both onstage and in the audience, queer and feminist theorists emphasized that desire flows back and forth between the stage and the house in ways that compel the exchange of 'looks' between actor and actor and between actors and spectators. Riffing off feminist film theory, particularly Laura Mulvey's landmark essay 'Visual Pleasure and Narrative Cinema' (1975), queer theatre and performance theorists promoted desire as a key force circulating in the exchange between performers and spectators that constitutes one of the most important elements of live performance. Because queer desire has always threatened the status quo, LGBTQ performance has often been censored, long after the Comstock Law and other laws against obscenity were defanged, most notoriously during the 1990s National Endowment for the Arts (NEA) Four scandal in the USA. During that dark moment for federal support of the arts, three queer performers – John Fleck, Tim Miller, and Holly Hughes – and one outré feminist performance provocateur – Karen Finley – found their grants rescinded by the NEA, even after a panel of their peers had voted to fund them. The subsequent protests and debates about public support for art that conservatives considered offensive raged for nearly a decade and deeply politicized many LGBTQ theatre and performance artists.

Queer desire was a central issue in this debacle, as politicians on the extreme right, most of whom never saw the work they condemned, insisted that taxpayers' money should not be spent supporting 'depraved' events. The debates pitted so-called normal citizens against artists whom conservatives deemed perverse and marginal according to 'community' standards of decency, applying obviously biased criteria that favoured conventional families produced in married, heterosexual relationships. The NEA scandal exemplifies how theatre and performance has always been a political hotbed, a site of deep contention over what it means to be a fully enfranchised citizen of a nation, and how sexuality has always been a primary consideration in these fraught debates.

Plays and productions: on and off Broadway

The place and moral propriety of non-heterosexual citizens has long been argued in theatre and performance, whether covertly, as in many pre-1969 commercial plays, or overtly, as in the autobiographical, avant-garde solo performances by LGBTQ performers popularized during the 1990s (see Dolan, 'Lesbian and Gay Drama,' 2005). *Boys in the Band* (Theater Four, New York, 1968), by Mart Crowley, was the prototypical pre-Stonewall gay play; it depicted the lives of gay men for a public audience from a stereotypical but sympathetic perspective for the first time. The play is about a group of friends gathering to celebrate the birthday of Harold, the most conspicuously 'queer' man among them. Harold's pock-marked face and his self-described Jewish aspect combine to physicalize the distaste mainstream audiences felt for homosexuals at the time. His unattractive countenance and his effeminate, 'limp-wristed' bearing confirmed the stereotype of gay men as ugly and feminine. The rest of Harold's circle and their interactions fit other cultural presumptions: the self-hating homosexual who has internalized the homophobia of his society and turned it on himself; the 'straight-acting' gay man who can pass as heterosexual; the promiscuity of gay male culture, based on what was seen as a constitutional inability to be monogamous; and the desire for sex over emotional intimacy.

The men's drunken revelry and the game of Truth or Dare that provides their entertainment inspire vicious accusations and painful confessions and revelations. The host's straight male college friend coincidentally looks him up that same evening and arrives at the party to confide problems with his marriage. Instead, his commitment to his heterosexual relationship is strengthened as the gay friends perform their pathos for him. Ultimately, *Boys in the Band* allows the characters and the play's spectators to see gay men through heterosexual eyes and pity or damn them accordingly. Despite what are now considered its retrograde politics – the characters are isolated in the bubble of their class, privileged by their whiteness, and completely ignorant about civil rights activism, and they admit they would be straight if they could be – the play ran for 1,000 performances off Broadway, was adapted for film by Crowley and directed by William Friedkin, and became a reference point for a generation who thought the story told them something true about gay male lives. In fact, it reinforced the representation of gay men as pathological, diseased, suicidal, and perverse.

In the early 1980s, before the discovery of what became known as HIV/AIDS, and as political acceptance for gay men and lesbians in the USA began to gather momentum, playwright/actor Harvey Fierstein took *Torch Song Trilogy* (Little Theatre, 1982) to Broadway after its various parts had been presented at downtown New York theatres such as La MaMa and the Actors' Playhouse beginning in 1978. Fierstein's play comprised three one-acts that told, from an affirming, sometimes campy perspective (an ironic style punctuated with heightened artificiality that some considered an aesthetic exclusive to gay men), stories about the peccadilloes of white gay male life in New York. In the solo play *International Stud*, Fierstein played Arnold Beckoff, a gay, Jewish New Yorker who is also a professional drag queen (not unlike Fierstein himself). As Beckoff, Fierstein imitated gay sex acts, describing his experience with an anonymous partner in a club. Although the moment probably marked the first simulation of anal sex in Broadway history, Fierstein's Jewish shtick made him familiar to New York audiences. His disarming, slightly self-deprecating comic style invited the audience to laugh with him rather than at him, and in the process to accept his differences. *Torch Song Trilogy* ran for 1,222 performances and won a Tony Award for Best Play. Fierstein went on to write the book for the successful musical *La Cage Aux Folles* (Palace Theater, New York, 1983), a comedy based on a French film about a female impersonator, his gay partner, his partner's son, and the heterosexual family into which this son intends to marry. Although it is full of slapstick humour, *La Cage* preaches tolerance and pride, ideas sanctified by the musical's long Broadway run of 1,761 performances.

Lesbians off Broadway: Jane Chambers

As these examples show, gradually, white gay men writing gay plays saw their work successfully produced in mainstream forums. No commercial counterpart existed at the time to tell the story of lesbian lives or those of LGBTQ people of colour. Not until 1980 did openly lesbian playwright Jane Chamber's *Last Summer at Bluefish Cove* receive a production at Westbeth Theatre in Greenwich Village, a small stage in the bowels of what was then the city's subsidized housing for artists near the West Side piers (although the production soon moved to the Actors' Playhouse). The play was produced by The Glines, an organization that championed gay theatre mostly for gay audiences rather than attempting to mainstream its content. Like *Boys in the Band*, *Bluefish Cove* relied on the realist dramatic formula that tried to insert the characters into a dominant form to tell stories of a marginalized subculture. Where Mart Crowley located his boys on the Upper West Side of Manhattan in a relatively moneyed environment, Chambers placed her lesbians in a beach vacation community that resembled Cherry Grove, a gay and lesbian summer spot on Fire Island, off Long Island, New York.

In *Bluefish Cove*, a group of lesbians vacation together to unwind, to celebrate their long-standing friendships, and to be themselves in one of the few places where they don't have to hide their sexuality. Most of the women share a dense history of sexual relationships with one another. The lightly bickering pairs establish themselves as 'typical', allowing Chambers to assimilate lesbians' lives into the familiar heterosexual model. All the women are coupled but one. Lil is the inveterate Don Juan, the senior member of their community who's had relationships with many of the friends gathered that summer but who is currently alone, recovering from an unspecified form of cancer. Although Chambers types the characters predictably – from the gruff butch to the mothering femme – their mutual affection and their commitment to their sustaining friendships provided one of the first positive, complex illustrations of lesbian community on stage.

After Chambers establishes the women's relationships, the play's plot is set in motion when a heterosexual woman, Eva, books the cottage next door for the summer, unaware she's renting in a lesbian enclave. Eva becomes a device through which Chambers teaches the audience about lesbians, as the spectators' eyes are opened along with the character's. At first, Eva is befuddled by the absence of men among the women she befriends, and she makes innocuous, naïve remarks that provide the play's comedy, along with its point of entry for heterosexual spectators. But Lil is enchanted by Eva. Her attraction to the straight woman, which Eva eventually reciprocates, brings Eva into the fold of lesbian community, even as Lil suffers the return of her cancer. In a formula typical of lesbian plays of the 1980s, the narrative trajectory belongs to the straight woman who finds her lesbian desire and comes out by the play's end. But in a twist that is also typical, Lil dies in *Bluefish Cove*, ostensibly of cancer, but symbolically because of her non-monogamous, masculine, tomcat behaviour, which threatened the normative, conventionalized, insistently coupled world of the play. Her great love for Eva comes too late; Lil's mortality allows her newly lesbian partner to go on to self-actualize alone. Chambers herself died of cancer in 1983, abruptly ending a career that never again saw the success of *Bluefish Cove* but that produced several other notable plays, including *The Last Snow* (Playwrights Horizons, New York, 1974), *My Blue Heaven* (The Glines, New York, 1982), and *Quintessential Image* (Women and Theatre Program Conference, Minneapolis, 1982).

Early LGBTQ venues

Many gay and lesbian theatre and performance theorists saw danger in realism's ideological entrenchment in insistently normative values that promote heterosexuality as the appropriate standard for the middle-class lives of American families, and whiteness as the default perspective from which drama speaks (see Dolan, *Presence and Desire*, 1993, and *Geographies of Learning*, 2001). As playwrights and directors tried to add lesbian and gay drama to the conventional American canon, escalating production costs obstructed their attempt at visibility and parity in commercial venues.

Some lesbian and gay theatre artists found other forums for their artistic visions, starting subcultural venues such as New York's Caffe Cino. Caffe Cino is often referred to as the coffeehouse where off-off Broadway began in the early 1960s, and it was one of the first places regularly to stage work by and about gay men. Owner Joe Cino was an idiosyncratic impresario who corralled his friends and acquaintances into performing on a stage so small it barely held three actors at one time. His café on Cornelia Street was a bohemian haunt, part of the coffeehouse culture in Greenwich Village in which artists, intellectuals, and political progressives flourished. The stage in the café's basement became for Cino a 'magic' space, almost sacred in how seriously he regarded the performances mounted there. Historian Wendell Stone, in his book *Caffe Cino: The Birthplace of Off-Off-Broadway* (2005), says that even if no one showed up to see a performance, Cino would insist that the cast 'do it for the room', because he felt 'the space had its own needs and powers' (p. 26). Many gay male playwrights who went on to some renown got their start at Caffe Cino, including Lanford Wilson, whose early play *The Madness of Lady Bright* (1964) – which concerned a rather tragic, lonely drag queen – became one of Cino's first successes. The musical *Dames at Sea* (1964) also premiered at Caffe Cino, starring the eighteen-year-old Bernadette Peters in a lead role. *Dames* spoofed Busby Berkeley musicals, using camp to gild its lyrics and choreography, and it proved to be Caffe Cino's most commercial success. Usually, the café attracted a coterie crowd; in fact, the artist Cino hired to create posters for performances at the café purposely made the graphics difficult to read so that only those spectators who knew what to look for would be able to decipher the information. The conservative politics of the early 1960s made such caution necessary.

The Drill Hall, the premiere LGBTQ theatre venue in London, was built in 1882 for a group of army riflemen and was used by Sergei Diaghilev in the early 1900s to rehearse his Ballet Russes with Vaslav Nijinsky. Since the 1980s, it has made its reputation by producing work 'led and illuminated by a gay, lesbian and queer aesthetic' (www.drillhall.co.uk/p45.html). The Drill Hall organized the Arts Lobby against Section 28 in the 1990s and now focuses its outreach on LGBTQ youth. The venue has produced solo performers and plays and performances by numerous gay and lesbian artists, in some ways translating the legacy of Caffe Cino in the UK. Buddies in Bad Times Theatre, in Toronto, Canada, was established in 1978 by three recently graduated York University students. When Matt Walk and Jerry Ciccoritti left the theatre shortly after, Sky Gilbert turned it into a professional gay theatre. It remains one of the most visible gay producing organizations in North America.

The WOW Café in New York's East Village (established in 1980) became a vital proving ground for a generation of lesbian performers who rejected the tenets of realism, the proscenium stage, and commercial theatre. WOW's core organizing collective decided early on not to apply for grants so that they wouldn't be beholden to anyone but their audiences and their own artistic collective for financial and creative support. People worked at WOW with few resources, in a 'poor theatre' style that lent their performances an edgy immediacy. Ticket prices were intentionally kept low to enable a range of spectators to attend performances. First housed in a long, narrow storefront on East 11th Street, the café soon moved to an old walk-up factory space on East 4th Street at the Bowery, where the theatre still makes its dusty home after purchasing the building from the city for $1 in the early 2000s and raising $125,000 to bring it up to state health and safety requirements (see Kate Davy, *Lady Dicks and Lesbian Brothers*, forthcoming). Nearly thirty years after it was founded, WOW maintains the same low-budget aesthetic and operating principles.

Holly Hughes at WOW

Performance artist and playwright Holly Hughes, who came to New York from Michigan in the early 1980s to be a visual artist, found herself at WOW instead. Disillusioned by the constraining political correctness she found in the feminist art world, Hughes revelled in WOW's anarchy and its refusal to toe anyone's party line. Hughes' underground classic *The Well of Horniness* (1983), whose title parodied

Radclyffe Hall's iconic lesbian novel *The Well of Loneliness* (1928), caused a sensation at WOW. Written as a radio play but originally performed live by artists who had already become infamous as part of WOW's core collective (Alina Troyano, Peggy Shaw, Sharon Jane Smith, and Hughes, among others), the play stages a parodic romp through lesbian subculture that quotes the conventions of radio drama, detective fiction, soap opera, melodrama, early television shows, and vaudeville. Because many spectators at WOW knew the performers, the insider crowd could laugh at how their friends performed with or against their own type. For instance, the rather demure and feminine Troyano performed a toughened male police sergeant in Hughes' *The Lady Dick* (WOW Café, 1984), while Hughes played the more conventionally feminine (if slightly insane) femme fatale.

Hughes also wrote the eloquent, absurdist lesbian duet *Dress Suits to Hire* (1987), which was performed by Peggy Shaw and Lois Weaver. The story takes place in a second-hand store above 2nd Avenue on Manhattan's Lower East Side, where two sisters spin out an evening of role-playing that crosses Genet's *The Maids* with Sam Shepard's *True West*. In poetic prose that refers to the myths of pioneering American spirit and infuses them with lesbian pathos and desire, Hughes created roles for Shaw and Weaver that let them play to their strengths but also stretched their repertoire. Weaver, for example, who always played the innocuous femme in her performances with Shaw – who was then her on- and offstage life partner – performed the character Michigan in *Dress Suits* as a sort of dominatrix, manipulating the surroundings and her companion's mental and emotional environment by creating generative – if perverse – fantasies. Shaw, known for her masculine, butch lesbian performances, played Deeluxe dressed like Rita Hayworth, wearing a form-fitting sheath dress and dangling earrings. Their highly eroticized exchanges and complexly gendered interactions made *Dress Suits* a tour-de-force of lesbian performance and writing.

After *Dress Suits*, Hughes wrote and toured autobiographical solo performance pieces, including the poetic *World Without End* (PS 122, New York. 1989), Hughes' reverie on her late mother; *Clit Notes* (PS 122, New York. 1994), a ribald comedy whose title couldn't be printed in most newspapers; and *Preaching to the Perverted* (New Conservatory Theatre, San Francisco, 1999; revised, PS 122, New York. 2000), an ironic, sardonic reflection on her entanglement with the Supreme Court in the NEA case. Hughes began as a manic presence onstage at WOW; as you watched her, it was hard to imagine what she might do next. Untrained as an actor, she refused to observe the theatre's proprieties and would regularly break the fourth wall to confront spectators directly with her cackling, unsettling, infectious laugh. Once she began a solo career, however, her monologues became more elegant and constrained. In *World Without End*, for example, Hughes sat in an oversized stuffed armchair to recount rueful stories about her relationship with her mother. *World Without End* and *Clit Notes* brought Hughes to the attention of Congress during the NEA Four debacle. *Preaching to the Perverted*, which she performed nearly ten years later, detailed Hughes' experience as a political pariah and the costs of being singled out for national disparagement as a lesbian performance artist. Always insightful and observant, the piece allowed Hughes a kind of vengeance, not just for her treatment at the hands of a so-called democracy but for the way even progressive colleagues failed to understand the costs of her notoriety in the NEA affair. Hughes now teaches at the University of Michigan, where she trains students in the Art Department how to break the rules of live performance.

Split Britches

The WOW Café spawned other lesbian solo performers and collectives. The Split Britches Company became WOW's sustaining force. Shaw, Weaver, and Deb Margolin began their work at WOW with their signature play, *Split Britches* (1982), an impressionistic homage to Weaver's reclusive female relatives in the Blue Ridge Mountains of Virginia. Shaw and Weaver founded the café on the heels of the Women's One World Festival they organized in 1980 and 1981. They took on leadership roles within the collective – Weaver by teaching acting, directing, and performance composition to WOW members, Shaw by providing unmitigated artistic and physical support for experimentation on WOW's boards. Twenty-five years after WOW was founded, Shaw recalled going to the theatre daily to sweep and wash the floors, donating her 'sweat equity' to keep the place running smoothly. She remembered her pride in having her own theatre to keep clean, so rare was it for lesbians (or any women, at the time) to control their own space (see Dolan, *Menopausal Gentleman*, forthcoming).

Margolin, Split Britches' heterosexual and Jewish member, wrote many of the troupe's performances, although they devised them collectively on the basis of their individual dreams and longings. Margolin brought her idiosyncratic presence to their performances in ways that, if they couldn't be called lesbian, could certainly be called queer (see Hart and Phelan, 'Queerer Than Thou', 1995; Dolan, 'Seeing Deb Margolin', 2008). Her writing for the troupe was impressionistic and poetic, and she refused to follow the conventional formulas of domestic realism. The refreshingly radical dramaturgy on display at WOW came from lesbian and feminist artists determined to fashion new forms for new contents and preoccupations. Together, Split Britches produced *Beauty and the Beast* (Avenue of the Streets, New York, 1982), *Upwardly Mobile Home* (WOW Café, New York, 1984), *Little Women: The Tragedy* (WOW Café, New York, 1988), and *Lesbians Who Kill* (The Club at La MaMa, New York, 1992).

Each performance poached from a range of references — from popular culture to high art, from Yiddish theatre to nineteenth-century melodrama, and from current events to myths and fictionalized stories personal to each member of the troupe. Each performance blended monologues and dialogue, often formed in non-sequiturs around the thinnest thread of plot, and imagistic language and numbers that evoked moods, ideas, and character more than they did a linear narrative. Each performance exemplified the troupe's spirit of dedicated abandon, the carefully structured anarchy of three women performing in public with all the heart, glee, and passion they could muster. Split Britches changed the face of LGBTQ theatre. By vehemently rejecting realism and its domestic concerns, they established a practice that some called 'lesbian camp' (see Davy, *Lady Dicks and Lesbian Brothers*) and encouraged parodies of dominant culture's conventional forms.

Eventually, Shaw, Weaver, and Margolin moved on to solo careers. On a whim, when Split Britches was invited to perform at Hampshire College and only Shaw was available, Shaw created her first solo piece, *You're Just Like My Father* (1993), in which she documents how her mother both warned her against her increasingly obvious sexual 'perversion' and enabled her daughter's masculinity, dressing her in Shaw's father's clothes and remarking on their similarities (see Dolan, *Menopausal Gentleman*). *Menopausal Gentleman* (Ohio Theatre, New York, 1997) is an elegiac monologue that narrates what it meant for Shaw to be a fifty-three-year-old grandmother who dressed and looked like a thirty-five-year-old man. Infused with rock and roll music of the 1950s and the butch stylings of lesbians unconcerned with politically correct sexuality, *Gentleman* showed Shaw in peak solo performance form even as she settled into her physical middle age. *To My Chagrin* (Jump Start, San Antonio, 2001) offered an autobiographical rendering of Shaw's relationship with her biracial 'grand-companion-son', Ian, and her determination to provide him with a proper masculine role model.

Must: The Inside Story (Wellcome Collection, 2008), co-written with Suzy Willson and produced with the UK's Clod Ensemble, is called 'a journey through the shadows of a city, a pound of flesh, a book of love' (frontispiece). The melancholic, highly imagistic and personal piece lets Shaw mine her memories by touring through her own ageing body, psyche, and soul. It is filled with quietude markedly different from Shaw's earlier, more raucous performances, and it seems to resolve something about the progress of her life: 'Forsythia bloomed three times this year. I can hear the unfamiliar sound of yellow in the winter woods and the quiet when the yellow freezes. The sound of time changes as I get older. I can hear the relaxing sound of my head clearing and my skin softening' (chapter 11). Shaw is tuned in to her body as it merges with the natural environment, instead of fighting, at her usually accelerated performance tempo, with her own differences.

Shaw and Weaver long represented the 'butch–femme' stylings of some lesbian self-presentations, in which each partner performs masculinity or femininity as a surface enactment of a gender role re-written across basically female anatomy (see Case, 'Towards a Butch-Femme Aesthetic', [1988] 2009). Where Shaw's solo work took her more deeply into a butch lesbian performance of herself that exemplifies scholar Judith Halberstam's definition of 'female masculinity' in her 1998 book of the same title, Weaver's solo shows detail her experiences as a theatrical femme. Her outsized femininity, which explodes the conventions of gender just as much as butch performance, emphasizes that even a gender performance that appears congruent with female anatomy is also what feminist theorist Mary Ann Doane called a masquerade ('Film and the Masquerade', 1982). Weaver first performed her femme persona Tammy WhyNot, a caricature of American country music singer Tammy Wynette, at the Club Chandalier on Avenue A in New York's East Village (1983), in a lesbian variety show called *Chit Chat with Carmelita* emceed by Alina Troyano in her Latina femme drag persona Carmelita Tropicana. With her big hair, Southern slang, and earnest Dolly Parton-esque delivery, Tammy became an instant hit on the lesbian performance scene. Weaver has perfected the persona over her career, from her first solo outing, *Faith and Dancing* (1996), to the continuing series *What Tammy Needs to Know* (since 2004), a 'trailer trash course' she offers as a performance workshop. In her position as Professor of Contemporary Performance Practice at Queen Mary, University of London, Weaver has turned towards using performance to address human rights issues broadly drawn. Her *Long Tables* project (since 2003) uses performance techniques to stage conversations about current political issues with a clear, applied, activist component. Her *Diary of a Domestic Terrorist* (since 2006) is an ongoing lecture-performance project that 'promotes the use of private details as a means of public resistance' (www. splitbritches.com/pages/lois.html).

Deb Margolin's solo career has also flourished, with *Carthieves! Joyrides!* (HERE Arts Center, New York, 1995), *O Wholly Night & Other Jewish Solecisms* (Jewish Museum of New York, 1996), and *Index to Idioms* (Kitchen Theatre, Ithaca, 2003), among other performances (see Dolan, 'Seeing Deb Margolin'). After the trio parted ways, Margolin was able to explore representations of her heterosexuality outside the inquiries into lesbian desire that had guided her career with Split Britches. Margolin's Jewishness, her deeply irreligious spirituality, and her foundational, radical humanism align her with performance styles and contents sympathetic to LGBTQ, as well as straight, concerns. Because her aesthetic incorporates Split Britches' dedication to devising performance through personal yet always political desires, Margolin's presence is rife with powerful testimony to feminist and Jewish political and spiritual experience rarely seen even in the relatively avant-garde world of performance.

Lesbian Brothers move into the mainstream

With Split Britches as the reigning example, WOW nurtured many notable collectives and solo performers, who often developed work at the café and then moved into other downtown Manhattan (and sometimes commercial) venues. The Five Lesbian Brothers (Lisa Kron, Peg Healey, Moe Angelos, Babs Davy, and Dominique Dibbell), for example, began their group performance career with *Voyage to Lesbos* (Wow Café, New York, 1989), a fantastical, parodic, episodic rendering of rampant, wild, completely unconventional sexual exploration. The contradiction of the group's name, which confounds conventional expectations of sexuality and gender, signals their challenge to decorum, and their insistently collective process flouts conventional theatre practice that demands writers, directors, and actors accomplish separate tasks. The Brothers devise, write, direct, and perform in their own work. After starting at WOW, they soon moved their base to New York Theatre Workshop (NYTW), an off-Broadway theatre a short way down East 4th Street from the café but a world away in terms of resources and public visibility. Their productions at NYTW included *Brave Smiles* (1992), a parody of genre films that stereotype lesbians; *The Secretaries* (1994), an outrageous take-off of killer lesbian horror films, in which a cabal of secretaries at a logging plant sacrifice local men in monthly rituals that coincide with their menstrual cycles; and *Brides of the Moon* (1997), a queer space odyssey that satirizes nuclear families and middle-brow American aspirations.

The Brothers' *Oedipus at Palm Springs* (NYTW, 2005) was a relatively slick production that loosely adapted Sophocles' original to tell a story about incest and the complexity of sexual desire set at a lesbian resort outside Palm Springs, California. The play employed the Brothers' broad, socially satirical style and poked fun at its own realism, but it also tried for the dramatic pathos of more serious drama (see Dolan, 'Blogging on Queer Connections in the Arts and the Five Lesbian Brothers', 2006). Although the production was critically well received, *Oedipus at Palm Springs*, like so much explicitly lesbian – as opposed to gay male – theatre, wasn't picked up for an extended run. This disappointed the collective, who want their work to achieve wider visibility. The Brothers maintain a loose affiliation, although most of them concentrate on solo performance or regional theatre work or have moved on to television and film or other careers.

The Brothers' Lisa Kron, for example, one of the early denizens of WOW, has toured American regional theatres with her autobiographical monologues *101 Humiliating Stories* (NYTW, 1994) and *2.5 Minute Ride* (La Jolla Playhouse, 1996). Produced by George C. Wolfe at the Joseph Papp Public Theater in New York in 1999, the Obie Award-winning *2.5 Minute Ride* tells a mournful story about Kron travelling to Auschwitz with her father, a survivor of the Holocaust, intercut with a rather absurd story about Kron bringing her lesbian partner to a family reunion at a large amusement park in Ohio. The visually simple, emotionally tender piece uses irony to soften the pain of revisiting the past and just as delicately (and with less camp than Harvey Fierstein used fifteen years earlier) mingles Kron's Jewish ethnicity with her lesbian identity.

Kron calls her breakout play, *Well*, a 'solo show with other people in it' (p. 16). First produced at the Public in 2004, *Well* moved to Broadway in 2006, where it ran for three months and was nominated for two Tony Awards. Although financially less than successful, *Well* stands as one of the few plays by a woman – let alone an out lesbian – produced on Broadway in the past fifty years. The play uses Kron's engaging, contemplative, ingenuous solo style to recall her years battling a mysterious health crisis that took her to a residential allergy clinic while her mother agitated to racially integrate the family's Lansing, Michigan, neighbourhood. 'Ann Kron', a character representing Lisa's mother (played by Jayne Houdyshell), cosily ensconced in her living room throughout the play, sits in a reclining armchair downstage left from which she comments on Lisa's reconstruction of their mutual story. Kron addresses the audience directly at key moments, and the handful of other actors in the play – several of whom are performers of colour – break character to share their opinions on the proceedings and eventually to rebel against Kron's authorship, siding instead with her mother. Kron moves from her mother to the others, trying to placate her collaborators and her audience and, at the same time, do justice to her own narrative, which addresses what it means to extricate yourself from a suffocating life to find your way. Lisa's self-exploration contrasts with Ann's personal and political efforts to address race relations in their Midwestern town. *Well*'s warm representation of Ann Kron and Lisa's mitigating presence as the audience's guide and confidante make the play a seductive, rueful, moving meditation on autonomy and need. The play's pointed theatricality also underlines the fact that personal memory and experience in US theatre have mostly been told through men's eyes. Introducing her play, Kron declares, 'I work using autobiographical material, but ultimately this is a theatrical exploration of a universal experience' (p. 17). Kron's claim that two women's experiences can represent the universal appears almost revolutionary, even in the twenty-first century, in a Broadway forum that usually offers centre stage literally and metaphorically to men.

From the avant-garde to commercial theatre

Gay male collectives, spaces, and solo performers

Gay men were less apt to form collectives like Split Britches or WOW through which to create theatre that explored their experience. Pomo Afro Homos (established in

San Francisco in 1991), a trio of African American gay men – Djola Bernard Branner, Brian Freeman, and Eric Gupton – toured performances in the early 1990s that investigated gay male and African American identity. When they took *Fierce Love: Stories from Black Gay Life* (Josie's Juice Joint, San Francisco, 1991) to Anchorage, Alaska, to perform at Out North, the local gay theatre, advertisements the theatre had intended to place on city buses were rejected and the mayor proposed that the Anchorage Assembly cancel the theatre's municipal grant. The Assembly unanimously rejected the idea, but the controversy reflected the early days of the culture wars around LGBTQ theatre and performance in the USA. Pomo Afro Homos' *Dark Fruit* (Public Theater, 1991) illustrates the social stigmas caused by both homophobia and racism in a series of vignettes that continually shift cultural perspectives. The piece works with irony, parody, and poignant optimism to describe the difficult pleasures of being gay men of colour. Brian Freeman also tours solo performances, including *Civil Sex* (Public Theater, 1997), a piece in which he plays Bayard Rustin, the first African American to participate in the civil rights struggle as an out gay man and an African American in the nascent gay rights movement. In 1999, he restaged the piece as a three-act play (www.audiologo.blogspot.com/2007/07/black-lgbt-theater-passin-it-on.html). Referencing black lesbian poet Audre Lorde's *Sister Outsider*, Freeman says, 'I sometimes feel like "Brother Outsider" as I struggle with what it means to move in from the margins. And it's the less-than-fabulous, the dark, complicated, and messy secrets of history that don't always make people heroes or saints that I find myself exploring now' (www.alpertawards.org/archive/winner99/freeman.html).

Although gay men in the 1980s and 1990s didn't foster their own version of the WOW Café, in 1980 queer performance artist Tim Miller co-founded PS 122 in New York's East Village. The venue became a home for LGBTQ as well as all other kinds of experimental and avant-garde performance. ('PS' originally stood for 'public school' in New York City's educational lexicon. When the building became available for re-use, the initials came to stand for 'Performance Space'.) In its heyday, PS 122 housed performances by Holly Hughes, Peggy Shaw, Lois Weaver, Deb Margolin, Alina Troyano, and other denizens of the Lower East Side scene, along with work by Miller and other gay male artists. In addition to PS 122, Miller co-founded Highways Performance Space and Gallery in Santa Monica in 1989 with critic Linda Frye Burnham. The venue supports work by white and of-colour gay men and lesbians.

One of the first openly gay male solo performance artists, Miller addresses gay civil liberties and sexual liberation through his monologue- and movement-based, activist, autobiographical work. He gained part of his renown as one of the NEA Four; his subsequent entanglement with the US justice system became fodder for his self-reflexive, politically dissident community-based work. Miller is also infamous for the signature nudity of his performances. In *My Queer Body* (Highways, Santa Monica, 1994), at the height of the HIV/AIDS pandemic, Miller disrobed and moved into the audience to interact with spectators. He sat on people's laps, talking openly and affectionately with strangers about what it meant to be a naked gay man inviting himself into close proximity with other people's bodies. Spectators, at first embarrassed, soon relaxed into and even applauded Miller's naked interactions, which purposely challenged the physical degradation associated with people with HIV/AIDS in the dominant culture stereotype. Miller's performance openly celebrated gay male sexuality at a time when the queer community was being ravaged by the loss of those dying from the disease. In another groundbreaking moment in *My Queer Body*, Miller directly addressed his penis, entreating it to 'get hard' as a way of celebrating sexuality's necessity to life rather than its association with death.

Miller's solo performances have always concerned the relationship of sexuality to life and the future, belying queer theorist Lee Edelman's argument in *No Future* (2004) that it's politically productive to see queer people as resolutely 'presentist' and therefore without a future structured by the heterosexual rituals of marriage and child-rearing. Although Miller has no children – unlike many gay men and lesbians in the late twentieth and early twenty-first centuries who have decided to have children, through adoption or assisted reproductive technologies – since his earliest perform-ances, beginning with *Buddy Systems* in 1986 in New York, he has articulated hope for the possibilities of the future. As a result of his long-term relationship with Australian novelist Alistair McCartney (author of *The End of the World Book*), Miller has focused since 1999 on marriage equality and immigration rights for bi-national LGBTQ couples. His most recent performances, *Glory Box* (Legion Arts, Cedar Rapids, Iowa, 1999), *Us* (7 Stages Theatre, Atlanta, 2003), and *1001 Beds* (New Conservatory Theatre, San Francisco, 2006), address and attempt to inspire political activism around what it means to be a queer couple who can't settle in the USA because one of them isn't a citizen. His perform-ances use different metaphors – a hope chest in one, musical theatre in another – and never skimp on details as he shares, often in floods of words and torrents of images, his personal memories and fantasies.

Much of Miller's performance opus refers to the AIDS pandemic, a social crisis that gay, lesbian, and queer thea-tre continues to address. William Hoffman wrote one of the first so-called AIDS plays, *As Is* (Lyceum Theatre, New York, 1985), a dark comedy about a gay man who learns to accept his HIV-positive lover 'as is'. Larry Kramer's real-ist play *The Normal Heart* (Public Theater, New York, 1985) solicits identifications with an ill gay man named Ned Weeks and exhorts gay and heterosexual spectators to express their outrage at the lack of public funding for AIDS research and virus intervention. Revived at the Public Theater in 2004, after the development of the drug 'cocktail' that puts HIV/AIDS into remission and reduces it to a chronic disease for many people, the play starred the openly bisexual actor Raúl Esparza as Weeks. The anger at government indifference at the onset of the HIV/AIDS pandemic still rings through the play, allowing it to retain its power as an activist political theatre experience.

Performance and LGBTQ personal narrative

Solo performance continues to appeal to gay men and lesbians, because even at the beginning of the twenty-first century, the few queer experiences accommodated by commercial theatre tend towards two-dimensional caricature or conventional assimilationist characters rather than full-fledged, complex investigations of the variety and multiplicity of LGBTQ lives. Autobiographical solo performance's monologue structure offers room to address difficult social truths and allows LGBTQ people to explore their similarities to one another, as well as their differences. The form enables the performer to testify to his or her personal experience and asks spectators to witness the performer's life publicly. Solo performance, happily, also requires less expensive sets, lighting, costumes, and props and, obviously, no other actors.

Queer people of colour also tend to succeed with the solo performance form, perhaps because they can better control the means of production and the specificity of their audiences. For example, Alina Troyano, an early member of WOW, creates solo performances that usually begin at theatres in lower Manhattan and go on to tour universities, colleges, and performance venues across the USA. Troyano's alter ego/persona, Carmelita Tropicana, buoys many gay, lesbian, or queer events, often serving as a witty and warm emcee for performance festivals or community political events. Troyano's solo show *Milk of Amnesia* (PS 122, New York, 1994) details her necessary forgetting and remembering (or literally reassembling) of her very early childhood in Cuba, prior to her immigration to the USA. She uses cross-gender impersonations to represent not only the differently masculine and feminine sides of herself and her culture but also the bi-national ethnic loyalties inspired by immigrant life. Her collaborative show *Chicas 2000* (PS 122, New York, 2000) is a less serious romp through pop culture forms in the tradition of early parodic work at WOW. Troyano received a 1999 Obie Award for Sustained Excellence in Performance.

Puerto Rican lesbian solo performer Marga Gomez, in her show *A Line around the Block* (Public Theater, New York, 1996), which she toured across the USA, impersonates members of her family and her multiple identifications with different cultures. She has also performed the solo shows *Long Island Iced Latina*, *Los Big Names*, *Memory Tricks*, and *Marga Gomez Is Pretty, Witty & Gay*. Her collaboration with Alina Troyano, *Single Wet Female* (New York Queer Arts Festival, 2002), took off from the 1992 film *Single White Female* starring Jennifer Jason Leigh as a white woman who answers an ad for a roommate, becomes obsessed with her new roomie, steals her identity, seduces then murders her boyfriend, and tries to murder her. Through the parodic queer Latina eyes of Gomez and Troyano, the relationship between the two women becomes both overtly homoerotic and completely foolish. Their satire unravels into the outlandish stories and fantastical plots of mixed identity and surprise for which both performers are known. In truly post-modern style, the shape of the narrative matters much less than the jokes along the way – sight gags and visual comedy that often play off stereotypes of whiteness that invert dominant cultural presumption.

Chicano queer playwright/performance artist Luis Alfaro usually doesn't play other characters in his poetic solo performances, but he describes the visceral experience of growing up gay in Los Angeles Mexican American culture. Alfaro uses his body literally and metaphorically in *Cuerpo Politizado (Politicized Body)* (X-Teresa, Mexico City, 1996). In his monologue 'A Mu-Mu Approaches', he stuffs into his mouth box after box of typical American junk food – miniature white cakes with chocolate icing – while a taped monologue describes the compromises necessary to assimilate into US life. In 'Bachelor Party', Alfaro drinks shots of tequila in quick succession, using the crisp, loud bang of the shot glass on a small table beside his microphone to punctuate the ironies of the stories he tells while he drains the bottle. Alfaro, who received a John D. and Catherine T. MacArthur Foundation 'Genius Award', co-directed with Diane Rodriguez the Latino Theatre Initiative at the Mark Taper Forum from the mid-1990s to 2005.

Queer gender performance

Transgender performer Kate Bornstein presaged the 'genderqueer' movement of the late twentieth and early twenty-first centuries in LGBTQ culture in the USA. Bornstein's performance *Hidden: A Gender* (Theatre Rhinoceros, San Francisco, 1989) documented her experiences as a male-to-female (MTF) transsexual who came out as trans in the late 1980s. Since then, 'trans' has become a short-hand term for people who describe themselves as cross-gender, whether or not they've had the sex-reassignment surgery that would officially categorize them as transsexual. When Bornstein announced her identity in the late 1980s, transpeople were still viewed suspiciously because of the political complications they presented to some members of the gay and lesbian community. For instance, the lauded Michigan Womyn's Music Festival, which was established in the late 1970s as a women-only, outdoor haven of alternative culture, adhered to a policy prohibiting anyone not born a woman from attending the week-long event in which thousands of participants camp out and listen to musicians and other performers share their work. Michigan's policy has become unpopular over the years. The larger lesbian community has found common cause with transmen – people born women who identify as men or perform their identities through masculine social codes – and genderqueers – people who prefer to keep their gender identities fluid and changing rather than pinned to what they consider a too-stable binary, essentialist definition dictated by dominant culture.

In fact, many transgender people seek out audiences eager to see them perform their new identities onstage. Moe Meyers once said that many people who've undergone sex-reassignment surgery find their new selves confirmed in performance ('I Dream of Jeannie', 1991). Such affirmations continue as trans performers achieve more and more popularity in communities around the USA and the UK, as if needing the spectators at a performance to legitimate and admire their gender performativity. 'Drag kings', for instance, are transmen who perform as men, wearing the accoutrements of masculinity in ways that make their theatricality obvious. The International Drag King Extravaganza (IDKE), inaugurated in 1999 in Columbus, Ohio, and conferences like it bring together scholars and artists in festivals of performance and conversation where drag kings refine their performance styles and discuss their strategies.

Drag kings seem more self-reflexive about their work than the earlier generation of drag queens – men performing as women – in whose footsteps they might be seen to follow (see Esther Newton, *Mother Camp*, 1979). Because their gender illusions flow from a less socially powerful position ('women') to a more condoned and empowered one (the privileges that accrue around 'men'), the performers enjoy talking about their work as social activism and teasing out its political implications (see Ji Hye Kim, 'Performing Female Masculinities at the Intersections of Gender, Class, Race, Ethnicity, and Sexuality', 2007). Drag kings perform primarily in bars, clubs, and other socially oriented, ad hoc performance spaces. Other trans performers, including Bornstein, have written more formal plays to be performed in more traditional theatres.

Autobiographical solo performance appeals to queer artists financially, as well as aesthetically and politically, because it's relatively inexpensive to present and easy to tour. The trade-off is that a generation of LGBTQ artists have generated work that really only they can perform. Their contribution to the archive of queer performance is fundamental and impressive, but too little of it can be mounted by other performers at other theatres, which means its shelf life is limited. Hughes' *The Well of Horniness* and some of the Five Lesbian Brothers' plays with more conventionally inhabitable characters have been produced with other casts in other locations. But much autobiographical solo performance is tied to the artists by whom it was generated and depends on their physical presence to be meaningful. Nevertheless, the work collects a deep archive of LGBTQ experience and insights, and it represents an impressive record of formal and narrative innovation.

LGBTQ plays in the commercial theatre

While solo performance offers a rich vein of lesbian and gay drama, other LGBTQ theatre artists soldier on in more conventional forms, determined to see their work produced, recognized, and recirculated through the medium of the text. Although some of these lesbian and gay writers, directors, and actors remain committed to the somewhat essentializing category of 'gay or lesbian play', for many commercially successful, visible artists, their gay identities haven't constrained or necessarily even shaped their artistic careers. Playwright Terrence McNally, for example, one of the first out gay white men to be accepted into mainstream American theatre, writes plays about gay men but also plays and librettos that have nothing to do with sexual identity. McNally wrote the book for the Broadway musical theatre adaptation of *The Full Monty* (Old Globe Theatre, San Diego, 2000), for example, the British film about a group of unemployed working-class men who decide to make money by staging their own striptease routine. McNally has succeeded with realist drama, placing his gay male characters in familiar domestic situations in which they suffer the traumas of coming out, illness, and death.

McNally's *Love! Valour! Compassion!* (Manhattan Theatre Club, New York, 1994), for example, narrates several gay male couples' annual vacations at the country home of their friend Gregory, a talented dancer. Much like Chambers' *Last Summer at Bluefish Cove*, the play constructs the friends' summer community through their relationships. After contriving a series of personal, artistic, and health crises – including an HIV-positive diagnosis, ageing and the loss of mobility, and acts of infidelity – the play describes in a bittersweet epilogue how the couples live out their time together in comfortable, domestic ways. The play uses nudity more as decoration than as activism. Late in the play, the men in *L!V!C!* gleefully disrobe to swim together in a pond on Gregory's property, a moment the production blessed with charming naturalness. This more aesthetic nudity contrasts with how Tim Miller wields his nakedness as a political tool in performance.

McNally's gay male relationship drama indicated how far LGBTQ theatre had come in fewer than thirty years from *Boys in the Band*, although its race and class implications remained disturbing. The men in *L!V!C!* are white and wealthy, except for the Latino dancer, Ramon, whose affair with Gregory's (blind) boyfriend momentarily disrupts the household. Although Ramon is eventually embraced by the group of friends and cast as the star of Gregory's autobiographical ballet, his naked, stereotypically well-endowed

body is objectified in performance, and his race is token-
ized. After opening at the Manhattan Theatre Club, *L!V!C!*
transferred successfully to Broadway, was made into a film,
and went on to enjoy a run in American regional theatres.

Lesbian drama, like drama by women in general, has been
less successful at finding its way into the most visible commercial venues. Nevertheless, although she's not yet seen
her work produced on Broadway, lesbian playwright Paula
Vogel has achieved success off Broadway and in regional
theatre. Her play *The Baltimore Waltz* (Circle Repertory
Theater, New York, 1992) starred the openly lesbian actor
Cherry Jones (who in 2009 and 2010 played the president
of the USA on the television drama *24*) and was directed
by openly lesbian Anne Bogart (Artistic Director of the
SITI Company). The play allegorically addresses Vogel's
brother's death from AIDS. In theatrical flights of comic
fantasy, Vogel's three-character play follows a brother and
sister on their whirlwind search through Europe for a cure
for 'Acquired Toilet-Seat Disease Syndrome', the sister's
sexually contracted disease, which turns out to be a dis-
placement of the brother's HIV/AIDS. Vogel's play *How I
Learned to Drive* (Vineyard Theatre, New York, 1997) won
the Pulitzer Prize in 1998, making Vogel the first out lesbian to win the award (openly gay playwright Tony Kushner
won the 1993 Pulitzer for *Angels in America*). *How I Learned
to Drive* narrates with sad nostalgia L'il Bit's sexual awak-
ening (or molestation, depending on one's perspective)
by her Uncle Peck, in a presentational yet nuanced style
that's moving and liberating. The play's content, which is

obliquely lesbian in certain pronominal uses and off-hand remarks, addresses sexual identity in powerful, ambivalent, poignant ways. Vogel extends *Drive* away from domestic realism – and even comments on it sardonically, making the family dinner table a scene of anarchy, misogyny, and lewdness rather than a hallowed setting for conventional family values – to illustrate the unwieldy enormity of desire.

Vogel's play *The Long Christmas Ride Home* (Trinity Repertory Company, Providence, RI, 2003) continues the story of a severely unhappy family; the parents' furiously fractured relationship, the father's affair with another woman, the grandparents' sharp neglect and disparagement, and the children's fear and pain are enacted with puppets created by Vogel's collaborator, Basil Twist. The play mixes Bunraku-style puppetry with Japanese No theatre effects, creating a stunning aesthetic experience of emotional brutality. Although the style is Brechtian and resists psychology, the play's wallop hits hard and vividly critiques the failures of nuclear family structures. The play moves back and forth in time, foretelling the future of the three children (represented as rod puppets and then by live actors when the characters are adults) as they sit trapped in the back seat of a car rocking with (and nearly overturned by) their parents' pitched battle.

Vogel serves as Chair of the Playwriting Department at the prestigious Yale School of Drama, but as a woman she remains outside a certain circle of influence. Gender continues to affect the reception of plays by lesbians, as few women – lesbian or not – see their work produced on Broadway or in London's West End. In contrast, the Broadway productions of gay playwright Tony Kushner's *Angels in America: A Gay Fantasia on National Themes* (*Part One: Millennium Approaches*, Mark Taper Forum, Los Angeles, 1990, and *Part Two: Perestroika*, Mark Taper Forum, Los Angeles, 1992) were heralded as prophetic. Critics agreed that the epic two-part play spoke with breathtaking scope and intellectual, political, and theatrical daring to the concerns of a country living through the AIDS pandemic and the presidency of Ronald Reagan during the 1980s. In a virtuosic narrative that combines high theatricality with dialogue that covers the most intimate and the most political territory, *Angels* addresses universal philosophical themes: the reasons for life and the nature of death, especially for gay men, who'd never before been the central characters in a serious, artful Broadway play.

Prior Walter suffers from HIV in the early 1980s, when AZT, the initial course of treatment, was as inaccessible and valuable as gold. He is abandoned by his faithless Jewish boyfriend, Louis Ironson. Their relationship intersects with the deteriorating marriage of Joe Pitt, a Mormon lawyer working for the conservative Senator Joseph McCarthy flunky Roy Cohn, and Joe's wife, Harper, who is slowly being driven mad by the unspoken fact that Joe is gay. Surrounding these two relationships – which overlap when Louis and Joe begin an affair and when Prior and Harper find themselves sharing hallucinations – are disquisitions on the progress of history, grounded in the philosophy of Walter Benjamin, and stories about Mormon expansion into the western American frontier.

Unlikely partnerships develop between characters that re-envision the meaning of kinship. For example, Joe's Mormon mother travels from Salt Lake City to Brooklyn when Joe confesses he's gay, and she soon meets Prior, for whom she comes to care physically and emotionally. Prior and Louis' African American friend Belize works as a nurse in the hospital where Roy Cohn is admitted suffering from end-stage AIDS. Belize cajoles the dying man into bequeathing his illegally acquired stash of AZT to Prior. Cohn is also visited by Ethel Rosenberg, whom he framed and sent to die in the electric chair. Ethel teases him emotionally and politically as Cohn confronts his death, and then says the Kaddish – the Jewish prayer for the dead – over his body. The play uses humour, intellectual debate, theatrical spectacle, and scenes between unexpectedly matched real and fictional characters to draw spectators into a revised vision of kinship in which gay men, Mormons, African Americans of Caribbean descent, and Jews find family together. The moving, thrilling epic became a touchstone for a generation of LGBTQ theatre artists.

Identity differences and access to production

Gender and race politics continue to operate in the reception of LGBTQ plays. As a white (albeit gay) male, Kushner's opportunities seem unlimited, while Vogel, as a white lesbian, still plies her trade at least one status level below, if Broadway and West End productions are considered the apogee of success in conventional theatre. Gay and lesbian playwrights of colour often find themselves even more compromised by a lack of social approbation and access.

Singapore-born Asian American playwright Chay Yew has produced his plays at regional theatres across the USA. But Yew's work has never received a Broadway production, even though it stages political and sexual, racial and ethnic inquiries similar to those through which Kushner and David Henry Hwang, Yew's heterosexual Asian American counterpart, have garnered wide acclaim. Yew's plays, such as *A Language of Their Own* (Public Theater, New York, 1995), lyrically evoke how gay and racial identity bump up against each other in subtly shaded scenes whose images suggest the hybrid nature of both Asian and American cultures. Written during the height of the HIV/AIDS crisis, *A Language of Their Own* addresses the relationship between two Asian American gay men, one HIV-positive, and their difficulties balancing intimacy with sexuality. Yew has recently turned more and more to directing other people's work, and he won the 2007 Obie Award for Direction.

Chicana playwright Cherríe Moraga, a prolific political essayist, poet, and activist, began her theatre career with *Giving Up the Ghost* (1984) at the Minneapolis-based lesbian feminist theatre At the Foot of the Mountain. *Ghost* is an evocative tone poem about a young butch Chicana lesbian in love with an older femme who comes to represent everything the younger woman idealizes about her Mexican ethnicity. In a fragmented, post-modern form that eschews structural coherence for singular visual and narrative images, the play evokes the social schizophrenia of binary distinctions between lesbian and straight, Chicana and white. Moraga rewrote the play in a more realist form later in her career and committed herself to more stylistically conventional structures to accommodate Chicano domestic dramas such as *Shadow of a Man* (Eureka Theater, San Francisco, 1990) and the more expressionist *Heroes and Saints* (Mission Theatre, San Francisco, 1992). Moraga holds an artist's residency at Stanford University – and, indeed, many LGBTQ playwrights and theatre artists rely on the resources of colleges and universities through teaching positions, artists' workshops, and performance tours.

Racial and ethnic distinctions contribute to differing degrees of visibility for much LGBTQ drama, theatre, and performance, although it would be misleading to draw a strict correlation between sexuality, race, and access to resource-rich, influential venues. For example, although he is an African American openly gay man, George Wolfe's artistic direction of the New York Shakespeare Festival/Public Theater from 1993 to 2004 regularly put his work among the most critically noticed theatre in New York. Wolfe demonstrated his commitment to racial, ethnic, and sexual diversity in the consistently varied seasons he directed or produced at the Public Theater, including plays by Chay Yew and solo performances by Marga Gomez and Lisa Kron, among many others. Under Wolfe's leadership, the Public regularly transferred work to Broadway, plays that typically included progressive themes and often addressed the lives and concerns of people of colour and gay men, whether or not they were marketed as gay or minoritarian. For example, Wolfe produced white gay playwright Richard Greenberg's *Take Me Out* (Donmar Warehouse, 2002; Public Theater, 2002), a play about a handsome, successful, and rather arrogant African American baseball player who suffers personal and professional consequences after he comes out as gay to his team and his fans. The production transferred from the Public to Broadway and received the Tony Award that year for Best Play. Its valentine to baseball as a metaphor for American democracy was as moving as the beautiful hero's adamant refusal to stay in the closet.

In fact, the 2003 Tony Awards in which *Take Me Out* got its nod demonstrated openly gay white men's incursion into the best-rewarded ranks of Broadway production. For example, when Marc Shaiman and Scott Wittman, the lyricists/composers of the musical adaptation of John Waters' 1988 film *Hairspray* (Neil Simon Theatre, New York, 2002), accepted their Tony Award for Best Original Score, the two men joked about the preponderance of gay and Jewish men in Broadway musical theatre and ended their speech with an affectionate kiss that was enthusiastically applauded by the audience. Of course, these two weren't the first gay men to collect accolades in American musical theatre (see Wolf, *A Problem Like Maria*). Composer/lyricist Stephen Sondheim, often considered the form's national treasure, now allows his gay identity to be part of his public persona. Sondheim's musicals rarely include gay themes – except, perhaps, for *Company* (Alvin Theatre, New York, 1970), which concerns the foibles of an unmarried man surrounded by insistently heterosexual, coupled friends.

Sondheim's example as a successful, openly gay man in an important, financially lucrative form illustrates that gay men and lesbians leave their imprint on all kinds of theatre production. Many white gay men, in fact, are noted theatre and film producers who bring gay and lesbian stories to more commercial forms. Scott Rudin produces highly marketable theatre and film productions, including John Patrick Shanley's play *Doubt* (Manhattan Theatre Club, 2004) on Broadway and the Academy Award-winning 2007 film adaptation of Cormac McCarthy's novel *No Country for Old Men*. Craig Zadan and Neil Meron are openly gay business partners responsible for producing the film adaptation of the musical *Hairspray* (2007). Their widely known sexuality doesn't seem to affect their business opportunities; on the other hand, their mainstream visibility and power don't guarantee that they'll advocate for other gay or lesbian artists, or that their own projects will be politically progressive. Once again, sexual identity guarantees very little.

Camp and drag performance

Queer camp traditions and gay male drag have long been a staple of US and UK performance and theatre, from performance artist Ethyl Eichelberger's 1970s and 1980s solo shows in New York, to the 1970s San Francisco drag queen group the Cockettes, who performed fantastical, glitter drag, to Hot Peaches, a drag troupe that travelled Europe in the 1970s. Playwright/performer Charles Busch is one of the avatars of off-off-Broadway female impersonation, writing parodic confections as vehicles for his own glamour drag. One of his earliest plays, *Vampire Lesbians of Sodom,* opened at Limbo Lounge in New York's East Village in 1984 and then ran for five years at the Provincetown Playhouse off Washington Square in Greenwich Village before he successfully expanded his career by writing comedy for heterosexual performers and mainstream audiences.

Other drag artists chose to remain downtown (literally and figuratively), as did Charles Ludlam and his Ridiculous Theatrical Company, which parodied high art and other cultural forms for twenty years at its Sheridan Square location in the Village. Ludlam and his business and life partner Everett Quinton regularly served up biting satires of sexual and social mores, queering melodramas such as *Camille* (Ridiculous Theatrical Company, New York, 1973) and a host of other genre conventions, as in the penny-dreadful, Gothic parody *The Mystery of Irma Vep* (Ridiculous Theatrical Company, New York, 1984), long a favourite on the regional theatre circuit. Ludlam performed in drag, but his costumes never completely hid his gender; he played Camille with his curly chest hair bristling purposefully out of his bodice. Ludlam wrote twenty-nine plays, all of which were produced at his theatre, and most of which he starred in and directed. His work, like much campy queer theatre, attracted a coterie crowd to his small basement theatre, but his plays' wit and intelligence and his performances' energy and charisma won him notoriety and respect far beyond the avant-garde.

Kiki and Herb began their own campy, gender-bending drag performances in San Francisco in the late 1980s, before moving to small Greenwich Village spaces such as the restaurant/bar the Cowgirl Hall of Fame and eventually to trendier clubs such as the Fez, on Manhattan's Lower East Side, in the late 1990s. They moved off Broadway to the

Cherry Lane Theatre to ply their unique theatrical pairing in a louche lounge act called *Kiki and Herb: Coup de Théâtre* (2003) that attracted larger, mixed audiences. Kiki (singer Justin Bond) is an elderly, past-her-prime torch singer, and Herb (musician Kenny Mellman) is her long-suffering accompanist. Although the thirty-something-year-old performers use no theatrical make-up to create age effects, they say that their characters are both over seventy years old. Their lounge act provides the occasion for stark commentary on the political moment, seasoned with fictional but strikingly realistic-sounding, bitter but poignant reminiscences from Kiki's constructed life that take on an eerie, sometimes hostile tone. What begins as light banter with her audience often descends into Kiki shrieking in anger, as Herb tries to follow along gamely on his keyboard. In 2007, *Kiki and Herb: Alive on Broadway* (Helen Hayes Theatre, New York, 2006) was nominated for a Tony Award for Best Special Theatrical Event, rather an understatement considering how unusual the pair would be on Broadway.

Belle Reprieve: LGBTQ theory into practice

Belle Reprieve puts theory and practice into conversation, as the play exemplifies the themes described in *Theatre & Sexuality*. In 1991, at London's Drill Hall, Lois Weaver and Peggy Shaw, of the US-based Split Britches troupe, and Bette Bourne and Paul Shaw, of the UK-based Bloolips, collaborated on a queer 'deconstruction' of Tennessee Williams' canonical play *A Streetcar Named Desire*. Written and produced on Broadway in 1947, *Streetcar* became a 'masterpiece' of American theatre. It won the Pulitzer Prize for Drama, ran for two years, and was made into a 1951 film directed by Elia Kazan starring Vivian Leigh, Kim Hunter, Karl Malden, and Marlon Brando. The play and the film exemplified the Method acting popular at the time, which strictly observes the conventions of fourth-wall realism and requires actors to access their characters and execute their roles with psychological, interior techniques. Since its debut, *Streetcar* has been taught in high schools and colleges around the world, perpetuating its international canonical status.

Williams' play takes place in a steamy, working-class apartment in New Orleans, where Stella lives with Stanley, her brute, emotionally inarticulate but physically and sexually powerful husband. Stella comes from upper-class Southern stock but turns her back on what was once a privileged existence when the family's estate, Belle Rêve (French for 'beautiful dream'), falls into disrepair and her relatives begin to die off. Leaving her older sister, Blanche, to contend with ageing relatives on the dilapidated estate, Stella moves to New Orleans, where she's entranced by Stanley's rough allure. When Blanche arrives in their small, ramshackle apartment unannounced, the clash between the sisters' former wealth and their current poverty creates sharp tensions between Blanche and Stanley.

Blanche disparages Stanley for his Polish ethnicity and his working-class manners and struts about his apartment putting on exaggerated airs. The frustrated Stanley digs into Blanche's past and learns that her snobbish façade conceals a more sordid existence. Blanche, it turns out, left Belle Rêve for a single-room-occupancy hotel, at which she accepted 'gentleman callers' who paid for her company. Stanley crushes Blanche's illusions, brutally raping her on the evening when Stella is taken to the hospital to give birth to his child. Stella returns to find her sister suffering a psychotic breakdown, her emotional and psychological damage finally beyond repair. In *Streetcar*'s final scene, doctors arrive from an asylum to take Blanche away, but her illusions return long enough to see the gentleman physician as a suitor come to court her. 'I've always relied on the kindness of strangers,' she famously remarks, as she takes his arm and is led out of Stanley's and Stella's lives.

Marlon Brando played Stanley on Broadway and in the film, becoming famous for his torn T-shirt, rippling muscles, and mumbling delivery of dialogue punctuated with echoing cries of 'Stella!!' as he called for his wife's ministrations. In the late 1940s and early 1950s, Brando epitomized American masculinity as the working-class stiff who proved himself with his muscles and his wits, surrounded himself with buddies in a tightly knit homosocial community, and expected his woman to service and sate his sexual needs. Against Brando's iconic white American manhood, Vivian Leigh played Blanche as a fading blonde beauty, just short of a caricature of fragile, mid-century white American womanhood taken to its hapless and helpless extreme. Their climactic confrontation remains one of the most famous scenes in theatre history, a date with destiny that exemplifies the triumph of masculinity over what Williams portrays as the manipulative wiles of female seduction.

Streetcar's hallowed place in the canon and its highly gendered meanings made it perfect for queer parody. *Belle Reprieve* appropriated the original to make its own case for gender performativity and theatre's complicity in inculcating conservative ideology about sexuality. Although the collaboration follows *Streetcar*'s basic plot, its vaudevillian form refuses to observe realist conventions. Instead, the four performers directly address the audience and don't even try to maintain the illusions of character. The scenery is two-dimensional, painted on cardboard flats that don't pretend to evoke a real 1940s apartment in New Orleans and instead refer to it in a critical, historical, Brechtian manner. Rather than using realistic dialogue, the characters often speak past one another, following two or three different narrative tracks simultaneously and interspersing their monologues with songs. Although each performer plays a character from Williams' original, they 'quote' their roles rather than fully taking on the character's psychological baggage or trying to conjure the character for the audience through emotional acting techniques. *Belle Reprieve*, in fact, is an exemplary post-modernist and Brechtian play and production that revels in revealing the operations of theatre and in its refusal to observe narrative unity or realist convention.

The actors' deconstruction of the original characters is evident from the cast list. Mitch (played by Paul Shaw) – Blanche's innocent, square suitor in the original – is 'a fairy disguised as a man' (Case, *Split Britches*, 1996, p. 150). The suggestion that Mitch is 'disguised as a man' refers to the common stereotype that gay men aren't real men, a slur that *Belle Reprieve* plays with and takes to a comic extreme. Likewise, Stella (played by Weaver) is 'a woman disguised as a woman' (p. 150), indicating that even an actor whose gender coincides with her character's sex is also masquerading rather than playing a role that's innate, natural, or true. Stanley is 'a butch lesbian' (played by Peggy Shaw, no relation to Paul). The troupe doesn't say that Stanley is *played by a butch lesbian*; Stanley, in this reading, *is* a butch lesbian. This claim allows spectators to detach his behaviour from common presumptions about masculinity being innate to men.

Instead, we see how masculinity plays, as a performance, on Peggy Shaw's body. Shaw doesn't hide the fact that she's a woman as she plays Stanley. Instead, she adopts the iconic masculinity he represents and plays it to the hilt, encouraging spectators to see that behaviour we consider masculine is learned, not inevitable, and can be adopted by anyone. Finally, Blanche is 'a man in a dress' (played by Bette Bourne, the famed drag queen of the Bloolips troupe). Femininity, too, is examined not as a set of innate qualities that inevitably stem from female anatomy but as a performance that any willing body can construct and parade.

The performativity demonstrated by these character/performer choices carries over into the play's décor. Instead of creating a set typical of domestic realism, which would faithfully represent the unkempt kitchen, bedraggled bedroom, and cramped bathroom that make up the tiny space in which Stanley and Stella live, *Belle Reprieve* presents the setting as exactly not real from the start. The stage directions indicate that '[t]he back drop is a scrim [a muslin cloth] painted to resemble the interior of a 1940s New Orleans apartment' (p. 150). Rather than a real stove, sink, tables, and chairs, *Belle Reprieve*'s set is a painting, a two-dimensional representation of a living space. 'Reality' is removed, second order, already distanced by being painted. The stage directions explain that '[t]hroughout the play, various painted cloth curtains are pulled ... to denote a change in scenery or mood' (p. 150). When the scene shifts to the bathroom, for example, a curtain is pulled on which is painted 'an oversized clawed foot of a bathtub and a straight razor lying on a tiled floor' (p. 157). When Stanley and Mitch prepare to play cards, Mitch carries on a painting of a card table, which he places over one of the several cardboard boxes used for the set (p. 161).

For the rape scene, 'the bathtub is removed and a painting of an oversized naked light bulb is pulled onstage' (p. 177), once again using two dimensions to signal the arrival of Blanche's moment of inexorable truth. These design choices continually remind spectators that no illusions will be created here. Instead, the actors play with the 'reality' constructed by Williams' original play, pointing out through their counter-choices that he, too, selected how to represent gendered relations in 1947 America. *Belle Reprieve* highlights theatre as a system of signification in which reality is obviously constructed and shouldn't be assumed to be natural, innate, or inevitable.

Belle Reprieve's very title plays on Belle Rêve, which in English productions of *Streetcar* is typically pronounced 'reev' rather than the French 'rehv'. The collaborators' version is peppered with Williams' dialogue throughout, as if to ground audiences' understanding in comparisons with the original. But, for the most part, the cast perform monologues, in counterpoint to dialogue, that have little to do with the overarching plot but that somehow set the mood for the ruminations on gender and sexuality that form *Belle Reprieve*'s core. The play opens with Mitch – the marginalized supporting player in the original – setting up the production's frame. He wheels on three large boxes, one of which will serve as Blanche's steamer trunk/hope chest, the other two carrying actors and transforming into other pieces of the set. He tells the audience that it's 4 a.m., when 'the thread that holds us to the earth is at its most slender, and all the creatures that never see sunlight come out to make mincemeat of well-laid plans' (p. 150).

Rather than providing the exposition of a conventional realist play, in which the characters' back-stories are presented to set the plot in motion, Mitch creates a mood of thoughtful reflection on things incongruous with what we suppose is 'normal'. Four o'clock is a liminal time between night and day, not quite dawn, when a queer netherworld of shapes and sounds circulate that don't resolve into sharply drawn images. Mitch describes '[d]arkness all around. Small sounds that give a taste of an atmosphere, a head turning, a body lit from behind, shadows in the dark, tiled hallway, a blues piano' (p. 150). He creates a tone more reminiscent of film noir than domestic realism, as if to suggest that underneath what looks like a family drama is a vein of criminality

65

with a mystery waiting to be solved. *Belle Reprieve* turns this into an enigma of gender and sexuality, and reveals how the crime of enforced and binary gender and compulsory heterosexuality hobbles our imaginations and our lives.

This noir ambiance and revisionary interpretation of *Streetcar*'s underlying meanings spin out in dialogue that refuses to unfold in a traditional linear style. After Mitch's establishing monologue, Stella appears, seductively drinking a bottle of Coke, to address the audience. She asks,

> Is there something you want? What can I do for you? Do you know who I am, what I feel, how I think? You want my body. My soul, my food, my bed, my skin, my hands? You want to touch me, hold me, lick me, smell me, eat me, have me? You think you need a little more time to decide? Well, you've got a little over an hour to have your fill. (p. 150)

She remarks directly on the spectators' act of looking at her, revealing the existence of the 'gaze' that feminist theorists have long argued is gendered male and operates to objectify the female body. Weaver/Stella addresses spectators' desire overtly, asking whether they want her, and for what. Like Mitch, she establishes a time frame, but if he sets the story at 4 a.m. – a point to which the characters continually refer, as though time isn't moving at all as the evening proceeds – Weaver/Stella announces that the production in which she performs will take just over an hour, time enough for spectators to decide what it is they want from the performers. The desire that courses between actor and spectator, which usually goes unremarked, is identified, claimed, and made part of the story that *Belle Reprieve* tells.

Within this revised mise en scène, Mitch and Stella nonetheless know in their bones how the story is supposed to play out. As Bourne/Blanche and Shaw/Stanley begin their speeches from inside the boxes Mitch has wheeled onstage, Stella says, 'I can usually feel it coming…' Mitch responds, 'Isn't there something you can do to stop it happening?… Change the script!' They continue:

> STELLA: Change the script. Ha ha. You want me to do what in these shoes? The script is not the problem. I've changed the script. … Look, I'm supposed to wander around in a state of narcotized sensuality. That's my part. (Blanche and Stanley speak simultaneously from inside the two largest boxes.)
>
> BLANCHE: You didn't see, Miss Stella, see what I saw, the long parade to the graveyard. The mortgage on the house, death is expensive, Miss Stella, death is expensive.
>
> STANLEY: Is that so? You don't say, hey Stella wasn't we happy before she showed up. Didn't we see those colored lights you and me. Didn't we see those colored lights.
>
> STELLA: And anyway, it's too late. It's already started. (p. 151)

As Blanche and Stanley speak lines lifted from the original play, the wheels of narrative that place the masculine, working-class Stanley at mortal odds with the carefully constructed, upper-crust but bitter, desiccating, feminine Blanche have started turning, and both performers emerge from their boxes ready to do battle. But because Shaw/Mitch and Weaver/Stella have already pointed at the theatrical apparatus for the gathered spectators by commenting on the inexorable plot and the operation of the gaze, the audience is alert to how this performance plays out before them, rather than watching with the same unthinking narcotized pleasure in which Stella languishes in a typical *Streetcar* production.

Belle Reprieve raids the pantry of Williams' play but uses its staples to cook up an entirely different meal. That Williams will be present but 'queered' is signalled by Blanche's very first line in this production: 'I've always depended on the strangeness of strangers' (p. 151), which literally perverts the original ('I've always depended on the kindness of strangers') and moves it from Blanche's valedictory speech to her very first. The world of *Belle Reprieve* is made strange indeed, but this new cast resignifies 'strange', just as the word 'queer' was reclaimed by 1990s activists from its derogatory, historically damaging connotations.

Belle Reprieve also resignifies territory and location. Just as within the play's world time stays fixed at the witching hour of 4 a.m., place, too, is caught in a nether land of queer import. When Bourne/Blanche bursts out of her box in her first scene, she says, 'Are we here? Is this the place? ... How sweet it is to arrive at a new place for the first time' (p. 152).

Stella regretfully informs her, 'Honey, we're in exactly the same place we started out from.' Blanche complains, 'I can't stand being in between. I just can't bear it.' Blanche's words might refer to her position as Williams' character, whose tragic flaw is her inability to see that she's trapped by a haunting, immobilizing past. But her words might also refer to the body of the drag queen who plays Blanche in *Belle Reprieve*. Bourne says in an interview,

> Who would not want to play Blanche? Yet I was always very keen to play her as a man in drag, and not try to be a woman. When I was living in drag it was very clear that I was a man – I wasn't passing as a woman. ... It was very important for me to be myself, in other words a man in a frock – a new idea about a man. I think men look great in frocks, and I don't really see that we have to impersonate women necessarily, so in that sense I'm not really a Drag Queen. (www.nyu.edu/classes/jeffreys/GayandLesbianPerformance/suellentrop/bloolips.html)

The spectator watching Bourne perform, after all, sees a person whose male anatomy is covered in female garb, playing at femininity with a body on which it might seem incongruous, given conventional expectations that femininity lines up neatly with femaleness. Bourne's liminality provides his pathos but also, finally, his liberation, as through this step-by-step refusal of realism's inevitable ravages, Bourne/

Blanche avoids the violent, devastating ending Williams wrote for the character.

Shaw/Stanley and Bourne/Blanche toy with the borders crossed in *Belle Reprieve* in a short early scene in which Shaw plays a guard who insists on seeing Bourne's passport. The audience has already been told the characters are in the same place they started; requesting travel documents underlines the fact that, in this play, 'borders' become metaphorical and once again refer to gender and appearance rather than geographical territory. Blanche says, 'Passport? I wasn't aware we were crossing any borders' (p. 153). Forced to produce papers, Bourne presents his passport but says his name is 'Blanche DuBois', which Stanley, playing the border guard, disputes. Blanche retorts, 'The information in that document is a convention which allows me to pass in the world without let or hindrance.' When Stanley says, 'You don't look anything like this photograph,' Blanche smoothly responds with a Wildean epigram: 'I believe nature is there to be improved upon' (p. 153). The exchange underlines the fact that Bourne/Blanche refuses to acquiesce to the naming conveniences of citizenship and improves on nature with a performance that belies 'manhood' and, by analogy, 'nation'.

Because *Belle Reprieve* refuses to take itself seriously, however, such meanings are playfully implied, while the performers/characters remind spectators that we're here to see a performance. Irritated with the exchange about passports and borders, Mitch says, 'Look, can't we just scrub 'round the search and get on with the scenes of brutal humiliation and sexual passion?' (p. 154). Once again, the characters know what's coming – unlike in realism, in which every performance attempts to make it look as though the events are happening for the first time. *Belle Reprieve* jettisons the conventional suspension of disbelief and replaces it with a more canny belief that performance itself can overturn the deforming ideological message realism usually delivers.

Belle Reprieve's dramaturgy also refuses conventional dialogue. In Act Two, Blanche ruminates on Stanley's sexuality while Stella simultaneously considers the pleasures of a good cold bottle of Coca-Cola. Although the two performers share the stage and speak consecutively, their lines don't refer to one another's thoughts. Instead, they seem to share a monologue that's moving on two different tracks simultaneously, undermining the import of both speeches. Whereas Stella's rhapsody on her Coke-drinking might be trivial, Blanche's debate about Stanley's sexuality is vital, but it is treated with the same light touch as the Coke question.

In fact, Stanley's realness is questioned throughout the play. Stella tells her husband, 'You don't satisfy me, you're not real.' 'Are you saying I'm not a real man?' Stanley blusters (p. 169), even after he's arm-wrestled with Mitch in a fever pitch of performed masculinity and homoerotic undertones, and sung the 1955 standard 'I'm a Man' to prove his virility in the show's performative context. But the enigma of Stanley's 'true gender' can't be resolved or expunged, as it most likely would be in conventional realism (see Dolan, '"Lesbian" Subjectivity in Realism', 1990). The mystery continues into *Belle Reprieve*'s second act, as

Blanche, the drag queen, soaks in the bathtub ('One day I'll probably just dissolve in the bath,' she reports. 'They'll come looking for me, but there'll be nothing left. "Drag Queen Dissolves in Bathtub", that'll be the headline' [p. 158]). As Mitch, the fairy, plays the ukulele on a step-ladder above her 'tub', Bourne/Blanche says,

> [T]here's something about Stanley I can't quite put my finger on. I can't put my finger on his smell. I don't believe he's a man. I question his sexuality. His postures are not real, don't seem to be coming from a true place. He's a pho-ney, and he's got her believing it, and if she has children he'll have them believe it and when he dies, they'll find out. ... Have you ever seen him naked? ... The noises he makes, the way he walks like Mae West, the sensual way he wears his clothes, this is no garage-mechanic working-class boy, this is planned behavior. This is calcu-lated sexuality, developed over years of picking up signals not necessarily genetic is what I'm try-ing to say. ... [W]hat I'm trying to say is, I think he's a fag. ... Only someone as skilled as I am at being a woman can pick up these subtle signs. (pp. 172–73)

As Blanche ponders, she leads the spectator to expect she will announce the supposed secret of Stanley's femaleness, which has in fact always been apparent to the characters, the performers, and the audience. Instead, Blanche announces Stanley is a 'fag', pronouncing queer sexuality as the 'open secret' of Stanley's difference and securing her revelation by asserting her own skill at 'being a woman', which, obviously, she is not. Bourne/Blanche's comic, elegant undermining of gender's authority derives from the layers of performance she teases out as constitutive of what we think we know when we perceive masculinity and femininity. No end looms in sight in this funhouse of many-gendered mirrors.

Belle Reprieve scores its insights into queer performativity and performance with a light touch, using vaudeville routines that also undermine realism's self-seriousness. In a set piece towards the end of the first act, Stella and Stanley rehearse a number reminiscent of the Marx Brothers, who drew many of their acts from vaudeville and burlesque. An extended play on 'what's funny' ('Show me what's funny.' 'You want me to show you what's funny.' 'Yeah, show me funny.' 'Okay, I'll show you funny … that's funny' [p. 166]) results in Stella ripping each of Stanley's sleeves in turn, spraying him with bottle of seltzer, and powdering him with a giant puff. Stanley gets his revenge when Stella is about to throw a pie in his face and he unexpectedly tips it into hers instead. This familiar comic routine, embedded in a rereading of *A Streetcar Named Desire*, signals that the four performers will avail themselves of any and all forms of culture to make their points.

In another burlesque-inspired scene, Shaw/Stanley stops the proceedings when he sees that Bourne/Blanche has her finger up her nose:

> STANLEY: Hold it, hold it ... Is there something I
> can help you with?
> BLANCHE: Please could you give me a tissue. I
> think I've got something stuck up my nose.
> STANLEY: Would you like me to have a look?
> BLANCHE: Please don't trouble. I think a tissue
> would probably do it. ... Probably a boogey, I
> expect. (p. 165)

Eventually, Mitch, too, gets involved in the examination, and the three of them stop the plot's thin thread to look closely and solicitously up Blanche's nose. They finally determine that what they've captured on the tissue looks 'like a piece of Christmas pudding' (p. 165); then the play continues. The performers use popular and middle-brow culture as equally fertile resources in *Belle Reprieve*. Forms such as vaudeville, burlesque, and conventional drama collide profitably as the production upsets audience expectations about the proper performance of gender roles and the traditional circulation of sexual desire.

Singing and dancing punctuate the production's vaudeville routines and dramatic turns. Each performer sings a song and delivers a monologue, as the play's material is distributed equally among them. This simple adjustment disputes realism's tendency to focus on the lead romantic couple and to use subplots to embellish what's typically a story about a man and a woman coming together or breaking apart. In *Belle Reprieve*, numerous stories replace the central Stanley–Blanche conflict as the narrative's resolute centre. Stanley and Stella, Stanley and Blanche, and Mitch and Blanche have their own 'dance breaks', moments when the performers improvise a few minutes of purely physical movement that isn't described or recorded in the script. Such breaks have become de rigueur in post-modern, avant-garde theatre. They interrupt the verbal text with a usually whimsical and nonsensical dance that seems to be about celebrating everyone's simple presence in the theatre at that moment. In *Belle Reprieve*, the dance breaks function in much the same way. They demonstrate relationships but also allow spectators to gaze on couples brought together for non-textual reasons, reasons more about performance and presence than story.

When *Belle Reprieve* approaches the climactic rape scene that prepares for the tragic end of *A Streetcar Named Desire*, the painted oversized naked light bulb is pulled across the stage. But the play doesn't proceed with the usual coerced seduction scene, in which Stanley is aggressive and crude and Blanche is fragile and undone; in *Belle Reprieve*, Stanley first appears blindfolded and delivers another monologue (one Shaw later recycled in her solo show *Menopausal Gentleman*). 'Don't panic', Shaw/Stanley urges spectators, as if to undercut the character's threat:

> Don't panic … I was born this way. I didn't learn it at theatre school. I was born butch. I'm so queer I don't even have to talk about it. It

> speaks for itself, it's not funny. Being butch isn't
> funny ... don't panic ... I fall to pieces in the night.
> I'm just thousands of other parts of other people
> all mashed into one body. I am not an original
> person. I take all these pieces, snatch them off
> the floor before they get swept under the bed,
> and I manufacture myself. (p. 177)

Shaw/Stanley reassures the audience by explaining that her fearsome masculinity is long-standing, constructed, and queered. She, the butch lesbian playing the furious working-class man, was 'born this way'. But when Shaw says she was 'born this way', she's referring to a performance of masculinity that's always already external rather than innate. She manufactures herself from pieces of other people that seem to fall from herself like scales from a fish. She becomes her masculinity by reassembling pieces of cultural detritus, the representations of gender through which she contrives her own performance. 'Peggy Shaw', she suggests, is no more real than 'Stanley Kowalski' in *Belle Reprieve* or in *A Streetcar Named Desire*. Any subject of ideology – fictional or 'real' – is manufactured by pieces of other people, a hopeful notion that suggests interconnectedness in our mutually found representations of our selves. Given such a reassuring confession, Shaw/Stanley further deconstructs him/herself and neutralizes the danger that the character represents in the original play.

In the final prelude to the rape scene, Mitch sings a song in the style of the Gershwins' 'The Man I Love', to which the other characters tap-dance in Chinese lantern costumes for unexplained reasons. As they dance, the number begins to fall apart, perhaps because they can't see out of their outfits. Stage directions indicate, 'The audience begins to hear them mumbling from under their costumes' (p. 178):

> BLANCHE: Oh, what are we doing? I can't stand it! I want to be in a real play! ... With real scenery! White telephones, French windows, a beginning, a middle and an end! This is the most confusing show I've ever been in. What's wrong with red plush? What's wrong with a theme and a plot we can all follow? ...
>
> STELLA: Now we all talked about this, and we decided that realism works against us. ...
>
> BLANCHE: But I felt better before, I could cope. All I had to do was learn my lines and not trip over the furniture. It was all so clear. And here we are romping about in the avant-garde and I don't know what else. I want my mother to come and have a good time. She's seventy-three for chrissake. You know she's expecting me to play Romeo before it's too late. What am I supposed to tell her? That I like being a drag-queen? She couldn't bear it. I know she couldn't. She wants me to be in something realistic, playing a real person with a real job, like on television. (p. 179)

With a nod to the critical debates about realism's effi-
cacy, the Pirandello-esque characters discuss their des-
tinies while hidden under Chinese lantern costumes.
Disembodied voices bemoan their fates in the avant-garde.
Bourne/Blanche's funny plaint offers a witty, ironic cri-
tique of realism, but the sad truth is that drag queens will
probably never be sanctioned to play real people with real
jobs on TV, let alone to perform as Romeo. Even the few
LGBTQ characters now represented on television in the
USA and the UK are rarely seen as real people with real
jobs. Too often still, they serve as foils for the heterosexual leads, as comic relief pitchers isolated from their own
communities.

Dared by Bourne/Blanche's dissatisfaction, the perform-
ers/characters agree to try realism. Shaw/Stanley goes for
broke: 'He opens [a] beer and shakes it, then lets it squirt all
over the stage, then pours some over his head before drinking it' (p. 179). But Bourne/Blanche barely lasts a moment.
As Shaw/Stanley becomes belligerent and physical and won't
let her pass through the room, she asks, 'Do we have to play
this scene?' (p. 180). As Stanley continues, Blanche takes off
one of her heels and threatens him. Stanley grabs her arm:

> STANLEY: Drop the stiletto!
> BLANCHE: You think I'm crazy or something?
> STANLEY: If you want to be in this play, you've
>   got to drop the stiletto.
> BLANCHE: If you want to be in this play you've
>   got to make me!

STANLEY: If you want to play a woman, the woman in this play gets raped and goes crazy in the end.

BLANCHE: I don't want to get raped and go crazy. I just wanted to wear a nice frock, and look at the shit they've given me! (p. 181)

Happily, Stella and Mitch intervene to pull the proceedings off track once again. They sing to Blanche and Stanley, reuniting the contentedly misbegotten couples.

Weaver/Stella ends *Belle Reprieve* with a coda reminiscent of Shakespeare's comedies. She asks the audience directly, 'Did you figure it out yet? Who's who, what's what, who gets what, where the toaster is plugged in? Did you get what you wanted?' (p. 182). But in this case, the story to unravel is told not just by words, but by the multiple, sometimes conflicting, contradictory, madcap, seriocomic, and sad narratives of gender, sexuality, and theatre written on these queer actors' bodies in performance. The play ends with an encore called 'I Love My Art':

I love the glamour, I love the drama,
I love I love I love my art
I love the glamour, I love the drama
I love I love I love my art. (p. 183)

Through artifice and camp, and by mining and then parodying Western theatre traditions from Shakespeare to the present, *Belle Reprieve* plays with gender and sexuality, undoing the dubious claim that our identities are natural or that we don't perform ourselves offstage as much as we do on.

New audiences: no longer preaching to the choir

Belle Reprieve represents only one kind of queer approach to theatre and performance, one that uses 'queer' in its verb form to deconstruct the legacy of drama that once made non-normative sexualities invisible (if not explicitly forbidden and demeaned). Although the play relies on spectators' knowledge of Williams' original to 'get' the performers' insertion of LGBTQ material, the performance also exemplifies the refusal to pin down sexual identity as singular and fixed that characterizes much queer theatre in the UK and the USA. While such post-modernist performance continues to find audiences who revel in its irreverent flouting of traditional theatre and conventional gender and sexuality roles, other LGBTQ performance creates a more realist and realistic archive of stories and experiences that reflect lesbian, gay, bisexual, transgender, and queer identities from bounded communities in different geographical locations. The myth of a transcendent LGBTQ community no longer pertains, since political representation and popular cultural images in the twenty-first century regularly demonstrate the diversity of our various lives, dreams, and desires.

This proliferation of performance styles, forms, contents, and audiences allows LGBTQ theatre to move into the next era of its development. Some explicitly gay-, lesbian-, or queer-identified venues remain active, including the long-lived Theatre Rhinoceros in San Francisco and Theatre Offensive in Boston (see Susan McCully, 'How Queer', 1997), as well as the WOW Café, Highways, and the Drill Hall. But the audiences they now attract are no longer made up exclusively of LGBTQ people. That is, although much LGBTQ theatre production began in communities where it mirrored the complications of people living as gay or lesbian Americans or Britons, this so-called preaching to the converted (see Miller and Román) no longer exclusively defines the creation or reception of lesbian and gay drama. By the twenty-first century, the criterion of 'authenticity', which once demanded that gay, lesbian, or queer experience be represented only by those who had lived it, gradually relaxed into a more open standard in which alternative sexual identity onstage or onscreen could be addressed, performed, and received by anyone. In the off-Broadway production *The Temperamentals* (The Barrow Group Studio Theatre, 2009, written by Jon Morans), for example, the history of Harry Hay's establishment of the Mattachine Society was performed by both gay and straight actors (including Michael Urie of the television series *Ugly Betty*, who had just recently come out as queer – the term on which he insisted instead of 'gay' – in *The Advocate*, the leading US LGBTQ magazine). The actors' sexual preferences were 'known' only through gossip, which had no bearing on the strength or believability of their performances. On the Showtime network series *Nurse Jackie*, a doctor, played by Eve Best, has fast and dirty sex in the hospital with a male nurse. As they frantically grope one another, he says, 'I have a girlfriend,' and she responds, 'So do I,' as they go on kissing. In the very next episode, Best's character welcomes her occasional girlfriend back into her life. Whether Best is lesbian or bisexual is entirely beside the point; the character she performs with such commitment and vitality provides a deliciously complex, fascinating, and funny role for a very skilled actor.

Community- or social movement-oriented theatre continues to sustain a diverse LGBTQ population, but lesbian, gay, trans, and queer drama, whether assimilationist or more radical, whether queer in content, intent, or form, more frequently disperses into the cultural mainstream. When Lisa Kron's *Well* played on Broadway (Longacre Theatre, 2006), for instance, the fact that Kron (or her director/collaborator, Leigh Silverman) is a lesbian (or Jewish, for that matter) was less salient than other aspects of the character she wrote and played, even though she and her character were completely open about their sexuality. *Milk*, the 2008 Academy Award-winning film about the political and personal life of Harvey Milk, the first openly gay elected official in the USA, was written and directed by two white gay men, but most of its gay male and lesbian characters were played by heterosexual actors, including Sean Penn, who played Milk, and James Franco, who played his lover. No one protested these casting choices as inauthentic or unbelievable; in fact, Penn won a Best Actor Oscar for his work.

It might seem paradoxical, but if the issue of who writes, directs, or performs LGBTQ roles or drama is less urgent than it was ten or twenty years ago, advocacy for LGBTQ artists to be recognized for their work in all avenues of the arts continues to be crucial. Presuming the power of 'arrival' can be a trap; that is, the past thirty years might demonstrate numerous changes in US and UK culture, but those decades also underscore the fact that change happens slowly and only by accretion. Political history demonstrates how easy it is for dominant culture to backslide into normativity as its default mode. Remarkably, the twenty-first century has provided impressive social gains for gay men, lesbians, bisexuals, and transpeople. A number of Western nations – including Canada, Spain, the Netherlands, South Africa, and Denmark – have legalized same-sex marriage, and many more, including the UK, have established domestic partnership or civil union policies. In the UK, where until 2003 Section 28 threatened the rights of gay people and those who taught or condoned gay subject matter, same-sex civil partnerships have been legal since 2004. In the USA, the Supreme Court decision to throw out the Texas sodomy laws; the legalization of same-sex marriages in Iowa, Vermont, Massachusetts, Connecticut, and New Hampshire, along with the passage of civil union legislation in many other states; even the decision of Wal-Mart, one of the country's largest, most politically conservative employers, to add sexual orientation to its anti-discrimination clause, all mark progressive change.

On the other hand, in spring 2010, New Jersey, despite being one of the more liberal states in the USA, voted against same-sex marriage, preserving what many see as the second-class status of civil unions for LGBTQ people. Transpeople across the USA continue to fight for their rights, struggling through a maze of city, state, and federal agencies that are often at odds over how or whether transpeople can revise the gender designation on their official documents. Brutal hate crimes against LGBTQ people continue to be reported; for only one example, Lawrence King, a fifteen-year-old transgender student in Oxnard, California, was shot and killed by a fellow high school student in 2008, allegedly because of his non-normative gender orientation. The Defense of Marriage Act signed into federal law by President Bill Clinton in 1996 continues to enforce compulsory heterosexuality and won't be overturned quickly or easily, given the intense political investments in its maintenance. After legalizing same-sex marriage in California through an appeal to the state Supreme Court in 2008, voters passed Proposition 8 just a few months later, which banned such unions by changing the state constitution to legalize marriage only between a man and a woman. The American religious right continues to finance and publicize these unjust maneuvers and to fulminate against all LGBTQ requests to authorize and legalize our relationships, inciting continual backlash against our social achievements. Numerous US politicians – according to the sobering documentary *Outrage* (2009, dir. Kirby Dick) – carefully construct closets that hide their own LGBTQ sexuality and use their power to legislate against queer people's rights so that no one will suspect their secret sexual preferences. And even liberal US presidents such as Barack Obama, as well as legislators, judges, and city administrators around the country, regardless of their personal beliefs, are loath to embrace the queer community's full sexual, racial, ethnic, and gendered diversity because they fear political reprisal.

LGBTQ issues too often land last on powerful politicians' priorities lists.

Given the precarious state of LGBTQ human rights and our hard-won but tenuous place in cultural representation, acute analysis and deep understanding remain crucial as political and critical strategies. I hope *Theatre & Sexuality* provides useful tools for thoughtful, ethical engagement, not just with LGBTQ performance, but with any theatrical, filmic, or televisual representations that teach us who we are and how to live with one another.

further reading

Gender often bifurcates LGBTQ theatre and performance scholarship. The earliest monographs and anthologies to cover the history of lesbians and gay men in theatre practice – such as Curtin's *We Can Always Call Them Bulgarians* (1987), de Jongh's *Not in Front of the Audience* (1992), and Clum's *Acting Gay* (1992) – treated the material from a decidedly male perspective. Even Sinfield's later *Out on Stage* (1999), his critical compendium of US and UK LGBTQ theatre, referred very little to lesbian performance. Lesbian and feminist projects, such as Case's edited collection of plays by Split Britches (1996) and my own *The Feminist Spectator as Critic* (1988) and *Presence and Desire* (1993), ameliorated this exclusion, but often focused solely on lesbian texts and productions.

The influence of post-structuralist and reception theories can be seen in the field's borrowings from film and television studies scholarship, such as Mulvey's 'Visual Pleasure

86

and Narrative Cinema' (1975), whose now-classic attention to the gendered gaze became useful for decoding sexuality differences in spectatorship. Doty's argument about 'seeing queerly' in *Making Things Perfectly Queer* (1993) incorporated reader-response theory and reception studies to suggest that anyone can practise the habits of 'queer' spectatorship without necessarily *being* queer. This shift from ontology – or a focus on being – to practices – that is, attention to what people *do* when they watch – became productive in thinking about LGBTQ theatre practice. Wolf's *A Problem Like Maria* (2002) offers a useful précis of LGBTQ reception theories and applies them to lesbian readings of popular, Broadway-produced American musical theatre.

Cultural history's importance to understanding LGBTQ theatre cannot be overstated. Schanke and Marra's *Passing Performances* (1998) describes LGBTQ artists in nineteenth- and twentieth-century theatre; Bernstein's *Cast Out* (2006) collects autobiographical reminiscences of lesbian and gay US theatre people; Bottoms' *Playing Underground* (2004) locates the US LGBTQ theatre movement within the off-off Broadway establishment flourishing concurrently in New York; Stone's history chronicles the memorable Caffe Cino (2005); and Román's *Acts of Intervention* (1998) describes the history of theatre and performance about HIV/AIDS. Chauncey's foundational *Gay New York* (1994), along with Duberman's oral history of the Stonewall rebellion (1993), and D'Emilio and Freedman's influential *Intimate Matters* (1988) relate lesbian and gay cultural history in which theatre and performance has had a major role.

Theory and criticism remain important to studying theatre and sexuality, alongside the plays and performances that constitute its archive. Savran's readings of Williams, Miller, and Inge, *Communists, Cowboys, and Queers* (1992), models how to reread the canon through the lens of sexuality; Phelan's *Unmarked* (1993) continues to influence contemporary queer performance theory; Sedgwick's *Epistemology of the Closet* (1990) and Butler's *Gender Trouble* (1990) lead new generations of scholars across disciplines to post-structuralist understandings of subjectivity; and Muñoz's *Disidentifications* (1999) and Arrizón's *Queering Mestizaje* (2006) apply these insights to the intersections of sexuality and race. Finally, Román's *Performance in America* (2005) incorporates LGBTQ theatre, solo performance, and queer reading and reception strategies into the history and contemporary practices of American theatre in the twentieth and twenty-first centuries, pointing towards its sometimes profitable absorption into a larger cultural scene.

Arrizón, Alicia. *Latina Performance: Traversing the Stage.* Bloomington: Indiana UP, 1999.

————. *Queering Mestizaje: Transculturation and Performance.* Ann Arbor: U of Michigan P, 2006.

Bernstein, Robin, ed. *Cast Out: Queer Lives in Theater.* Ann Arbor: U of Michigan P, 2006.

Bonney, Jo. *Extreme Exposure: An Anthology of Solo Texts from the Twentieth Century.* New York: Theatre Communications Group, 1999.

Bottoms, Stephen J. *Playing Underground: A Critical History of the 1960s Off-Off Broadway Movement.* Ann Arbor: U of Michigan P, 2004.

Butler, Judith. *Gender Trouble.* New York: Routledge, 1990.

Case, Sue-Ellen. *The Domain-Matrix: Performing Lesbian at the End of Print Culture*. Bloomington: Indiana UP, 1999.

———, ed. *Split Britches: Lesbian Practice/Feminist Performance*. New York: Routledge, 1996.

———. 'Towards a Butch-Femme Aesthetic' [1988]. Rpt. in *Feminist and Queer Performance: Critical Strategies*. Ed. Sue-Ellen Case. New York: Palgrave Macmillan, 2009. 31–48.

Chauncey, George. *Gay New York: Gender, Urban Culture, and the Makings of the Gay World, 1890–1940*. New York: Basic Books, 1994.

Cleto, Fabio, ed. *Camp: Queer Aesthetics and the Performing Subject, A Reader*. Ann Arbor: U of Michigan P, 1999.

Clum, John. *Acting Gay: Male Homosexuality in Modern Drama*. New York: Columbia UP, 1992.

———. *Something for the Boys: Musical Theatre and Gay Culture*. New York: St. Martin's, 1999.

———. *Staging Gay Lives: An Anthology of Contemporary Gay Theatre*. Boulder, CO: Westview, 1996.

———. *Still Acting Gay: Male Homosexuality in Modern Drama*. Updated edition. New York: St. Martin's, 2000.

Curb, Rosemary, ed. *Amazon All Stars: Thirteen Lesbian Plays, with Essays and Interviews*. New York: Applause, 1996.

Curtin, Kaier. *We Can Always Call Them Bulgarians: The Emergence of Lesbians and Gay Men on the American Stage*. Boston, MA: Alyson, 1987.

Davis, Jill, ed. *Lesbian Plays*. London: Methuen, 1987.

Davy, Kate. *Lady Dicks and Lesbian Brothers: Staging the Unimaginable at the WOW Café Theatre*. Ann Arbor: U of Michigan P, forthcoming.

de Jongh, Nicholas. *Not in Front of the Audience: Homosexuality on Stage*. Hoboken, NJ: Taylor & Francis, 1992.

D'Emilio, John, and Estelle B. Freedman. *Intimate Matters: A History of Sexuality in America*. Chicago, IL: U of Chicago P, 1988.

Doane, Mary Ann. 'Film and the Masquerade: Theorising the Female Spectator.' *Screen* 23 (1982): 74–87.

Dolan, Jill. 'Blogging on Queer Connections in the Arts and the Five Lesbian Brothers.' *GLQ: A Journal of Lesbian and Gay Studies* 12.3 (2006): 491–506.

Dolan, Jill. *The Feminist Spectator as Critic*. Ann Arbor: UMI Research P, 1988. Rpt. U of Michigan P, 1991.

————. *Geographies of Learning: Theory and Practice, Activism and Performance*. Middleton, CT: Wesleyan UP, 2001.

————. 'Lesbian and Gay Drama.' *A Companion to 20th Century American Drama*. Ed. David Krasner. Malden, MA: Blackwell, 2005. 486–503.

————. '"Lesbian" Subjectivity in Realism: Dragging at the Margins of Structure and Ideology.' *Performing Feminisms*. Ed. Sue-Ellen Case. Baltimore, MD: Johns Hopkins UP, 1990. 40–53.

————, ed. *Menopausal Gentleman: Peggy Shaw, Solo Performances*. Ann Arbor: U of Michigan P, forthcoming.

————. *Presence and Desire: Essays on Gender, Sexuality, Performance*. Ann Arbor: U of Michigan P, 1993.

————. 'Seeing Deb Margolin: Ontological Vandalism and Radical Amazement.' Introduction to Deb Margolin's *Index to Idioms*, and 'A Slave to Synaesthesia,' an interview with Margolin. *TDR: The Journal of Performance Studies* 52.3 (2008): 98–117.

————. *Utopia in Performance: Finding Hope at the Theatre*. Ann Arbor: U of Michigan P, 2005.

Doty, Alexander. *Making Things Perfectly Queer: Interpreting Mass Culture*. Minneapolis: U of Minnesota P, 1993.

Duberman, Martin. *Stonewall*. New York: Penguin, 1993.

Edelman, Lee. *No Future: Queer Theory and the Death Drive*. Durham, NC: Duke UP, 2004.

Fisher, James, ed. *'We Will Be Citizens': New Essays on Gay and Lesbian Theatre*. Jefferson, NC: McFarland, 2008.

Five Lesbian Brothers. *The Five Lesbian Brothers: Four Plays*. New York: Theatre Communications Group, 2000.

Freeman, Sandra. *Putting Your Daughters on the Stage: Lesbian Theatre from the 1970s to the 1990s*. London: Cassell, 1997.

Goddard, Lynette. *Staging Black Feminisms: Identity, Politics, Performance*. New York: Palgrave Macmillan, 2007.

Goodman, Lizbeth. *The Routledge Reader in Gender and Performance*. New York: Routledge, 2002.

Halberstam, Judith. *Female Masculinity*. Durham, NC: Duke UP, 1998.

Harbin, Billy J., Kim Marra, and Robert A. Schanke, eds. *The Gay and Lesbian Theatrical Legacy: A Biographical Dictionary of Major Figures* in *American Stage History in the Pre-Stonewall Era*. Ann Arbor: U of Michigan P, 2005.

Hart, Lynda. *Between the Body and the Flesh: Performing Sadomasochism*. New York: Columbia UP, 1998.

————. *Fatal Women: Lesbian Sexuality and the Mark of Aggression*. Princeton, NJ: Princeton UP, 1994.

Hart, Lynda, and Peggy Phelan. 'Queerer Than Thou: Being and Deb Margolin.' *Theatre Journal* 47.2 (1995): 269–82.

Hodges, Ben, ed. *Forbidden Acts: Pioneering Gay and Lesbian Plays of the Twentieth Century*. New York: Applause, 2003.

Hoffman, William. *Gay Plays: The First Collection*. New York: Avon, 1979.

Hughes, Holly. *Clit Notes: A Sapphic Sampler*. New York: Grove, 1996.

Kim, Ji Hye. 'Performing Female Masculinities at the Intersections of Gender, Class, Race, Ethnicity, and Sexuality.' Diss. University of Texas at Austin, 2007.

Kron, Lisa. *2.5 Minute Ride and 101 Humiliating Stories*. New York: Theatre Communications Group, 2001.

————. *Well*. New York: Theatre Communications Group, 2006.

Marra, Kim, and Robert A. Schanke, eds. *Staging Desire: Queer Readings of American Theater History*. Ann Arbor: U of Michigan P, 2002.

Martin, Carol, ed. *Sourcebook on Feminist Theatre and Performance: On and Beyond the Stage*. New York: Routledge, 1996.

McCully, Susan. 'How Queer: Race, Gender and the Politics of Production in Contemporary Gay Lesbian and Queer Theatre.' Diss. University of Wisconsin-Madison, 1997.

Meyers, Morris. '"I Dream of Jeannie": Transsexual Striptease as Scientific Display.' *TDR: The Journal of Performance Studies* 35.1 (1991): 25–42.

Miller, D. A. *Place for Us: Essay on the Broadway Musical*. Cambridge, MA: Harvard UP, 1998.

Miller, Lynn, Jacqueline Taylor, and Heather Carver, eds. *Voices Made Flesh: Performing Women's Autobiography*. Madison: U of Wisconsin P, 2003.

Miller, Tim. *Body Blows: Six Performances*. Madison: U of Wisconsin P, 2002.

Miller, Tim. *1001 Beds: Performances, Essays, and Travels*. Madison: U of
Wisconsin P, 2006.

Miller, Tim, and David Román. 'Preaching to the Converted.' *Theatre
Journal* 47.2 (1995): 169–88.

Minwalla, Framji, and Alisa Solmon, eds. *The Queerest Art: Essays on
Lesbian and Gay Theatre*. New York: New York UP, 2002.

Mulvey, Laura. 'Visual Pleasure and Narrative Cinema.' *Screen* 16.3
(1975): 6–18.

Muñoz, José Esteban. *Disidentifications: Queers of Color and the Performance
of Politics*. Minneapolis: U of Minnesota P, 1999.

———. '"Memory Performance": Luis Alfaro's Cuerpo Politizado.'
Corpus Delecti: Performance Art of the Americas. Ed. Coco Fusco. New
York: Routledge, 2000. 97–113.

Newton, Esther. *Mother Camp: Female Impersonators in America*. Chicago,
IL: U of Chicago P, 1979.

Phelan, Peggy. *Unmarked: The Politics of Performance*. New York:
Routledge, 1993.

Román, David. *Acts of Intervention: Performance, Gay Culture, and AIDS*.
Bloomington: Indiana UP, 1998.

———. *Performance in America: Contemporary U.S. Culture and the
Performing Arts*. Durham, NC: Duke UP, 2005.

Román, David, and Holly Hughes, eds. *O Solo Homo: The New Queer
Performance*. New York: Grove, 1998.

Savran, David. *Communists, Cowboys, and Queers: The Politics of Masculinity
in the Work of Arthur Miller and Tennessee Williams*. Minneapolis: U
of Minnesota P, 1992.

———. *A Queer Sort of Materialism: Recontextualizing American Theater*.
Ann Arbor: U of Michigan P, 2003.

Schanke, Robert A., and Kim Marra, eds. *Passing Performances: Queer
Readings of Leading Players in American Theater History*. Ann Arbor:
U of Michigan P, 1998.

Sedgwick, Eve Kosofsky. *Epistemology of the Closet*. Berkeley: U of
California P, 1990.

Shewey, Don, ed. *Out Front: Contemporary Gay and Lesbian Plays*.
New York: Grove, 1988.

Sinfield, Alan. *Out on Stage: Lesbian and Gay Theatre in the Twentieth
Century*. New Haven, CT: Yale UP, 1999.

Stone, Wendell. *Caffe Cino: The Birthplace of Off-Off-Broadway*. Carbondale: South Illinois UP, 2005.

Troyano, Alina, with Ela Troyano and Uzi Parnes, edited by Chon Noriega. *I, Carmelita Tropicana: Performing between Cultures*. Boston, MA: Beacon, 2000.

Wilson, James. '"Ladies and Gentlemen, People Die": The Uncomfortable Performances of Kiki and Herb.' *'We Will Be Citizens': New Essays on Gay and Lesbian Theatre*. Ed. James Fisher. Jefferson, NC: McFarland, 2008. 194–212.

Wolf, Stacy. '"Defying Gravity": Queer Conventions in the Musical *Wicked*.' *Theatre Journal* 60.1 (2008): 1–21.

———. *A Problem Like Maria: Gender and Sexuality in the American Musical*. Ann Arbor: U of Michigan P, 2002.

index

acknowledgements

Thanks, first, to Jen Harvie and Dan Rebellato, whose superb editorship of the Theatre & series has made it such a valuable contribution to the field; I'm flattered to be part of their list. Even a short book requires a great deal of support and assistance, sometimes more than a long one, because writing short requires you to crystallize your thoughts and choose each word carefully. Many people helped me meet this challenge. Adrienne Brown provided skilful, efficient research assistance and never scoffed at my sometimes silly requests. David Savran's generous reading helped improve and sharpen my thoughts and my prose. I appreciated Kate Haines' detailed editorial supervision at Palgrave, and the meticulous copyediting and production work by Vidhya Jayaprakash and team. Cathy Hannabach produced a very fine index within a very short turnaround time; I appreciate her scrupulous attention to my words (And thanks to Gayle Salamon for connecting me with

Cathy). Holly Hughes' assistance with fact-checking made my life easier and reminded me of my pleasure seeing, reading, and teaching her performances. The redoubtable duo Lois Weaver and Peggy Shaw (and the Bloolips fellows) allowed me to engage at length with *Belle Reprieve*, which makes me laugh out loud with astonishment and glee at its wit and insight each time I read it. Tim Miller's foreword is a great honour and caps many years of mutual admiration, respect, and love.

Thanks to Wiley-Blackwell for permission to substantially revise and incorporate into this book my essay 'Lesbian and Gay Drama' from David Krasner, ed., *A Companion to Twentieth-Century America Drama* (2005), 486–503, and to Peggy Shaw, Lois Weaver, Bette Bourne, and Paul Shaw for permission to extract chunks of *Belle Reprieve*.

Thanks to every LGBTQ and LGBTQ-friendly artist I mention in this book – as well as those space limitations forced to me leave out – for creating the performance history about which I feel so privileged to write. Finally, thanks to my students, past, present, and future, for their unflagging interest in LGBTQ theatre and performance and their willingness to encounter it and engage with it, regardless of the initials under which they hang their own identities. *Theatre & Sexuality* is written for all of them … and all of you.